PROFILES

one event six people

ABRAHAM LINCOLN

MATHEW BRADY

FREDERICK DOUGLASS

THE CIVIL WAR

ROBERT E. LEE

CLARA BARTON

GEORGE McCLELLAN

By Aaron Rosenberg

SCHOLASTIC INC.

New York Toronto London Auckland
Sydney Mexico City New Delhi Hong Kong

———

CONTENTS

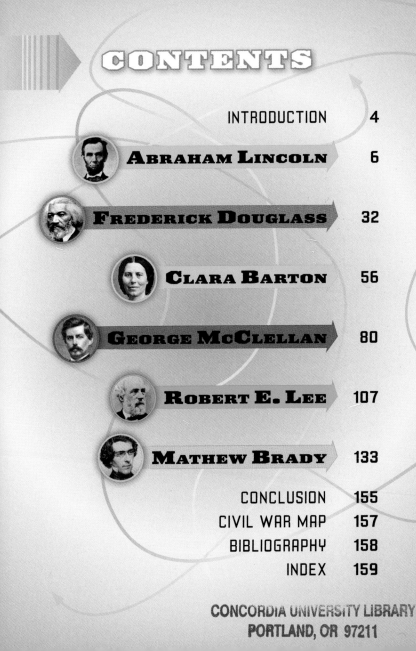

INTRODUCTION

THE AMERICAN CIVIL WAR BEGAN ON APRIL 12, 1861, when Fort Sumter in South Carolina was attacked. The attackers were soldiers from the Confederate States of America. Those eleven states had seceded from the United States of America. They had announced that they were now a separate nation. And then they declared war on the United States, or the Union.

The Civil War raged for almost exactly four years. It officially ended on April 9, 1865, when the Confederate army surrendered to the Union at Appomattox Court House in Virginia.

There have been two world wars and several other major wars since then, but the Civil War still took more American lives than any other war before or since. More than six hundred thousand soldiers died, and no one knows how many civilians (people who weren't in the military) were killed.

You can pick up a history book or go online to learn the basic facts about the Civil War battles. But who were the key people involved in the conflict? Everyone knows who Abraham Lincoln was. But did you know that he was president for the entire Civil War? Robert

E. Lee is famous as the Confederate general. But did you know that he was originally supposed to command the Union army? Who was Frederick Douglass, and why did Lincoln listen to him so closely? How did Clara Barton influence men and women on both sides of the war? Why is George McClellan important if he was actually dismissed from his military position? Who was Mathew Brady and why did Lincoln sometimes say he owed his entire presidency to him?

Throughout history, it's taken more than one person to win or lose a war or bring about dramatic changes. The six people in this book aren't solely responsible for the events surrounding the Civil War, but they are all considered major players during those events. And they definitely each had a hand in the outcome. We'll see who each of those people were, what their lives were like, and where they intersected each other. We'll find out how they influenced each other and the course of events, both during and after the war, and how they affected the entire country and everyone in it. Each of these people had a lasting influence. We are still feeling the effects of their actions, and their lives, today.

ABRAHAM LINCOLN

ABRAHAM LINCOLN was the sixteenth president of the United States. He is best known for his leadership throughout the Civil War and for his untimely death shortly after the war ended.

EARLY LIFE

ABRAHAM LINCOLN WAS BORN ON FEBRUARY 12, 1809, IN a log cabin in Hardin County, Kentucky. His father, Thomas, was a talented carpenter and made enough money to buy several farms in the area. Lincoln had an older sister named Sarah. He also had a younger brother named Thomas, who died while only a baby.

When Lincoln was seven, his family moved to Indiana. One reason they moved was because it was easier to buy land in Indiana. But Indiana also had

Cabin where Lincoln lived as a child

Artist's rendition of Lincoln as a boy

laws forbidding slavery. The Lincolns were Baptists, and their church did not approve of slavery. Some states allowed it and others did not. Slavery had been legal in Kentucky, and that had made the Lincolns uncomfortable.

In Indiana, the Lincolns lived near Little Pigeon Creek in Perry County. It was a wild countryside, filled with bears and other animals and overgrown with woods. Lincoln grew up learning how to raise crops, tend to animals, and cut down trees. People were not required to go to school back then. Outside of towns and cities, children only went when they could take time away from their chores. Only a few ever finished school. Lincoln was no exception. He attended several schools, but never for very long—there were always tasks to do on the farm, and he couldn't take the time away to study. He did learn to read, write, and do basic math, but nothing more. The rest of his knowledge was practical information, learned from his father and from hard work.

Lincoln's mother, Nancy Hanks Lincoln, died when he was nine. His father remarried the following year. Lincoln adored his stepmother, Sarah Bush Johnston. The two of them were very close. Sarah had three children of her own, so now the Lincolns were seven in all.

Sarah Bush Johnston

Lincoln grew up tall and strong— he was six feet four inches at his full height, towering over most men. He showed an early talent for storytelling and a thirst for adventure. When he was a teen, he and his friend Allen piloted a boat of produce down the Ohio and Mississippi rivers to New Orleans. It was the first time Lincoln had seen a city, and he loved the bustle and activity of it all.

GROWING UP

In 1830 Thomas Lincoln moved his family from Indiana to Coles County, Illinois. Abraham Lincoln was twenty-one by then. He was a grown man. He decided not to go with his father and stepmother.

Instead he sailed a canoe down the Sangamon River to New Salem. Lincoln was now on his own for the first time in his life.

He quickly found a job working for a businessman named Denton Offutt. Lincoln and two friends ferried Offutt's goods from New Salem to New Orleans. Offutt was so impressed he put Lincoln in charge of the mill and the store he had just set up in New Salem.

The job soon lost its appeal, and Lincoln searched for other work. He tried several different things, but none of them really suited him. He served as New

Lincoln ferrying goods from New Salem

Salem's postmaster for a time. He worked as the county's deputy surveyor. He bought a store of his own with a friend, though that business left Lincoln in debt after his partner died suddenly. He even served in the military! Lincoln was in the Black Hawk War of 1832. The war lasted three months, as American soldiers fought against Native Americans led by the war chief Black Hawk. Lincoln didn't play a big part in the conflict, but he was elected captain of his volunteer company. That was the first time anyone recognized his natural gift for leadership. It would not be the last.

POLITICS

Two months before the Black Hawk War, in March 1832, Lincoln had decided to try yet another new career. He wanted to be a politician! He ran for a seat in the Illinois General Assembly, which was the state legislature. Lincoln was well liked in New Salem, but most successful politicians had education, money, and influential supporters. Lincoln didn't have any of these. He ran anyway, and came in eighth out of thirteen candidates. There were only four seats, so he didn't win any of them.

Two years later, Lincoln tried again. This time he

won! He became a member of the legislature and joined the Whig political party (his father had also been a Whig). The party believed in developing the country and using modern techniques to help improve everyone's lives. Lincoln was all for this idea. His platform in 1832 had focused on clearing streams and building roads to help people in the farthest reaches of the counties. He had grown up a farmer, and knew what difficult work it was. Because of that, Lincoln had no problem supporting plans to modernize farms and make life easier and more rewarding for farmers.

Politicians did not have to be lawyers, but Lincoln decided he should know the law if he was going to help write new ones. He taught himself law, and in 1836 he was admitted to the bar, which meant he could legally practice. He moved to Springfield, Illinois, that same year and began his new life as a lawyer. Lincoln was smart, confident, and

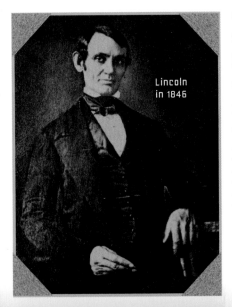

Lincoln in 1846

fierce. He soon became successful. His new skills made him a better politician as well. He served four terms in the Illinois House of Representatives. He finally stepped down in 1841.

That was not the end of Lincoln's political career, however. In 1846 he was elected to the U.S. House of Representatives. He only served one term there. He spoke out against the Mexican-American War during that time. Lincoln did not really object to the war itself, but he felt the way it had come about violated the Constitution and its laws. Unfortunately, the president, James K. Polk, supported the war. So did a lot of people around the country, including many of Lincoln's constituents in Illinois. Lincoln's statements about the war cost him a great deal of his political support. He did not run for Congress again.

Instead, he returned to Springfield and his law practice. Lincoln had other distractions now as well. In 1842 he had married Mary Todd, a young woman from a wealthy family in Lexington,

Lincoln's home in Springfield, Illinois

Kentucky. They had actually met in 1839 and had gotten engaged around Christmas of that year, but then had split up in 1841. They reconnected the following year and got married in early November. The Lincolns' first child, Robert, was born in 1843, and his younger brother, Edward, came along in 1846. The Lincolns had two more sons, William (Willie) in 1850 and Tad in 1853. Sadly, Edward died at the age of three and Willie died when he was eleven. Tad passed away at the age of eighteen. Only Robert survived to become an adult and have children of his own.

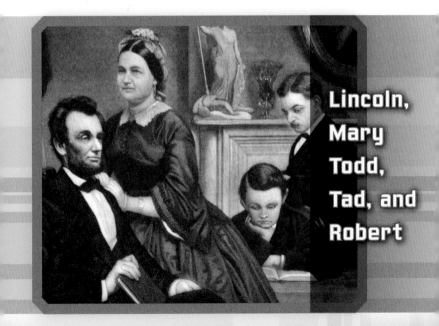

Lincoln, Mary Todd, Tad, and Robert

BACK TO POLITICS

In 1854 Congress passed the Kansas-Nebraska Act. This law canceled the Missouri Compromise of 1820, which had limited slavery to those states below the southern border of the Missouri Territory, as well as Missouri itself. The Kansas-Nebraska Act allowed each state in those territories to decide for itself whether or not it would allow slavery. Lincoln was horrified and outraged.

He decided that he could not stand by while the government allowed slavery to spread to the rest of the states. Lincoln ran for a position in the U.S. Senate at

Map showing the territories of Kansas and Nebraska in 1854

the end of 1854. His fame as a lawyer and his speeches against slavery had won him respect, and he did well in the early voting. But another candidate, Lyman Trumbull, who was also against the Kansas-Nebraska Act, won.

The Whig Party had begun to fall apart around this time. Half of the party supported the Kansas-Nebraska Act and half opposed it. They just couldn't agree. Finally the party collapsed. Lincoln and several others worked to bring together former Whigs. They also included politicians who were not happy with any of the other existing parties. Together they formed the

LINCOLN'S THOUGHTS ON SLAVERY

Lincoln had never approved of slavery. And the more he saw of it, the less he liked it. On October 16, 1954, he delivered a speech in Peoria, Illinois, in which he said:

"I cannot but hate it. I hate it because of the monstrous injustice of slavery itself. I hate it because it deprives our republican example of its just influence in the world—enables the enemies of free institutions, with plausibility, to taunt us as hypocrites—causes the real friends of freedom to doubt our sincerity, and especially because it forces so many really good men amongst ourselves into an open war with the very fundamental principles of civil liberty."

TO BE SOLD, on board the Ship *Bance Island*, on tuesday the 6th of *May* next, at *Ashley Ferry*, a choice cargo of about 250 fine healthy

NEGROES,

just arrived from the Windward & Rice Coast. —The utmost care has already been taken, and shall be continued, to keep them free from the least danger of being infected with the SMALL-POX, no boat having been on board, and all other communication with people from *Charles-Town* prevented.

Austin, Laurens, & Appleby.

N. B. Full one Half of the above Negroes have had the SMALL-POX in their own Country.

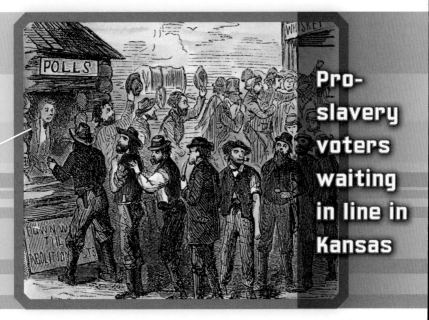

Pro-slavery voters waiting in line in Kansas

Republican Party. The Republican Party held its first
convention in 1856 to select its candidates for president
and vice president. Lincoln came in a close second for
vice president.

THE NATIONAL STAGE

Two years later, Lincoln campaigned for a seat in the
U.S. Senate. His opponent was Stephen A. Douglas.
Douglas was a Democrat and one of the most influen-
tial men in Congress. He had championed the Kansas-
Nebraska Act. Douglas didn't necessarily support

slavery, but he felt each state should decide for itself. Lincoln disagreed. "'A house divided against itself cannot stand,'" he told the Republican Party on June 16, 1858. It was a quote from the Bible.

```
I believe this government cannot endure
permanently half slave and half free. I
do not expect the Union to be dissolved—I
do not expect the house to fall—but I do
expect it will cease to be divided. It will
become all one thing, or all the other.
```

Lincoln and Douglas had a series of debates during the campaign for the Senate. Everyone wanted to see these two powerful, charismatic men argue about slavery and government. The debates became famous. Douglas won the election, but it was a close call. And now the entire nation knew Lincoln's name.

In early 1860 Lincoln set his sights on an even higher position than U.S. senator—he decided to run for president, with Hannibal Hamlin as vice president. Republican Party leaders in New York invited him to speak at Cooper Union on February 27, and Lincoln accepted. The Republicans held their convention on

May 18 in Chicago. Another politician, William H. Seward, was the favorite at the start of the convention. But Seward was too loud and outspoken to appeal to some of the party. Lincoln was more moderate in his views and his behavior. After three ballots, he won the party nomination.

Lincoln was up against Douglas for the second time, because the Northern Democrats had selected Douglas as their presidential candidate. Eleven of the Southern states refused to support Douglas, however.

The Lincoln and Douglas debates

Campaign poster of Lincoln and Hamlin

They walked out of the Democratic convention, and later selected their own candidate, John C. Breckinridge. A third party, the Constitutional Union Party, put forth its own candidate, John Bell. Douglas, Breckinridge, and Bell all campaigned hard and gave speeches across the country. Lincoln did not. He let the Republican Party handle the campaign instead. They produced leaflets, posters, pamphlets, and editorials. They had thousands of speakers talking to the country on Lincoln's behalf. They focused on his modest upbringing. They pointed out that only in America could a man rise from being a poor farm boy to become the president of the United States. In the end, Lincoln won the election, with a little over 1,800,000 votes!

THE CONFEDERACY

The Southern states hated the idea of Lincoln as president. Many of them depended upon slavery to run their farms and plantations, and Lincoln was openly against slavery. They knew he would never allow them to continue to keep slaves. Something had to be done.

South Carolina was the first state to secede from the Union, on December 20, 1860. By February 1, 1861, Florida, Mississippi, Alabama, Georgia, Louisiana, and Texas had also seceded. The seven states declared that they were now a separate nation called the Confederate States of America. They selected Jefferson Davis as their president on February 9.

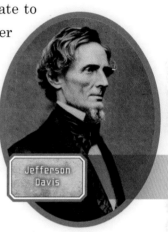

Jefferson Davis

Lincoln officially took office as president on March 4, 1861. One of his first acts concerned Fort Sumter. The military fort was in South Carolina, the state that had led the secession. Lincoln knew he either had to evacuate the soldiers there or send fresh supplies. He didn't want a war, but he knew he couldn't back down, either.

Lincoln knew he had an obligation to defend the United States and every property belonging to that Union, so he chose to send supplies to Fort Sumter. Lincoln sent Union soldiers to make sure the supplies got there safely. The Confederate army attacked the Union soldiers on April 12. The Civil War had begun.

WARTIME PRESIDENT

Lincoln had no military training and very little military experience. He had never actually seen combat during the Black Hawk War. But he took an active part in planning and running Union activities during the war. It was his decision to supply Fort Sumter. After the attack, Lincoln ordered a blockade of the Southern

The attack on Fort Sumter

ports to keep the Confederate army from getting supplies. He also issued a call for volunteers to enlist in the army. As the president, Lincoln was the commander in chief of the Union forces. One of his responsibilities was appointing the general in chief, who commanded the military and answered directly to the president. Lincoln knew that the choice of commander was critical to the war's success. Throughout the war, he demonstrated that he had no problem replacing that commander when he felt the man was not performing his duties properly.

Initially, Winfield Scott was given the position of commander, but Scott felt the best plan was simply to tighten the blockade and squeeze the South until they surrendered. Lincoln disagreed and overruled Scott, ordering the Union troops to advance. Though this led to their defeat at Bull Run, Lincoln continued to believe the only way to win the war was to attack the Confederates. He simply needed the right approach— and the right general.

After Scott resigned in 1861, Lincoln appointed George McClellan. McClellan proved to be a disappointment, however. He was too cautious and missed several key opportunities to attack, even though his forces outnumbered the opponent's. Lincoln removed him a year later, to be followed by Ambrose E. Burnside, Joseph Hooker, and Henry W. Halleck. Next, Lincoln promoted George Gordon Meade. Meade was in command during the Battle of Gettysburg on July 1, 1863. It was the bloodiest battle of the entire war. Over three thousand Union soldiers died, and another twenty thousand were wounded, captured, or missing at the battle's end. Lincoln was horrified by the death toll. On November 19 the Soldiers' National Cemetery at Gettysburg opened, which became the final resting place of all the soldiers who had died there. Lincoln attended the dedication. While he was there, he delivered his Gettysburg Address urging people to stay strong and focused on the greater good, and on the dream of living in a united, free nation once more. This speech became one of the best-known in U.S. history. A few months later, in March 1864, he replaced Meade with Ulysses S. Grant. This proved to be Lincoln's best choice yet, and Grant remained in command for the rest of the war.

Ulysses S. Grant

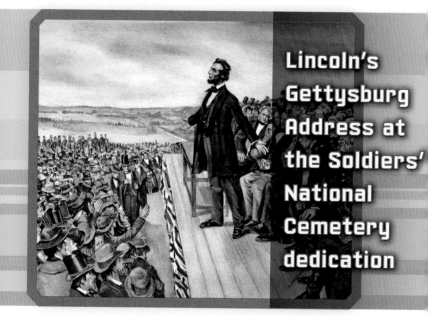

Lincoln's Gettysburg Address at the Soldiers' National Cemetery dedication

By July 1861, the Confederacy had grown. Virginia, North Carolina, Tennessee, and Arkansas had all seceded and joined the Confederate States of America. Missouri, Kentucky, and Maryland threatened to follow but did not. Part of the reason they stayed in the Union was because Lincoln negotiated with each state's leaders to keep them happy. He also arrested anyone inciting riots or secession; on September 24, 1862, he suspended habeas corpus, which meant the government could now arrest anyone without trial. They arrested between ten thousand and fifteen thousand people over the next few years. The Democrats accused Lincoln of becoming a tyrant, but he never became a dictator. He always allowed both his opponents and the press to have their say, even if it was only to criticize him. And Lincoln never considered postponing or canceling the presidential election of 1864, even when he thought he might lose.

EMANCIPATION

Lincoln was still debating what to do about slavery. His first concern was preserving the Union as much as possible. He had always disapproved of slavery,

but he would have let the Southern states keep their slaves if that could have held the Union together. Once the war began, that was not an option. Slavery became the central issue of the war. But Lincoln still had to find the right way to get rid of slavery. Otherwise he risked making matters worse and dividing what was left of the Union.

On September 22, 1862, Lincoln announced the Emancipation Proclamation. It officially went into effect on January 1, 1863. The proclamation freed any slaves in the Confederate states. Unfortunately, it did not say anything about slaves in Union states. And of course the Confederate states refused to acknowledge Lincoln's authority! The proclamation did mean, however, that slaves who escaped the South and reached the Union became free. And any slave the Union army found in Confederate territory was also free and got help fleeing to someplace more secure.

WAR'S END

Ulysses S. Grant was a powerful military commander, and for the first time, Lincoln sat back and stopped issuing orders to his generals.

Instead, he concentrated on getting reelected as president. He won the Republican Party nomination easily, and accepted Tennessee War Democrat Andrew Johnson as his running mate. Lincoln was worried that he might not get reelected. But he was determined to settle the matter of the war. He secretly promised to defeat the Confederacy before leaving office.

The Democrats chose Lincoln's former general in

Lincoln's second inaugural address

chief George B. McClellan as their candidate. But McClellan supported the war even though his party claimed it was a failure and a mistake. In September, Union general William Tecumseh Sherman seized Atlanta, which had been a major Confederate stronghold. This major victory boosted Lincoln's popularity, and he won reelection easily.

On March 4, 1865, Lincoln gave his second inaugural address. He could see that the war was almost over.

On April 9, 1865, Confederate general in chief Robert E. Lee surrendered his troops to Grant at Appomattox Court House in Virginia. It was the final blow to the Confederacy. The remaining rebel armies followed Lee's lead over the next few months. By June 23, 1865, the war was finally over.

NO TIME LEFT

On April 14, 1865, Lincoln and his wife attended the play *Our American Cousin* at Ford's Theatre in Washington, D.C. Unfortunately, an actor and Confederate spy named John Wilkes Booth had learned of the president's plans. Booth hated the idea of emancipation, and he had decided to kill Lincoln. Booth crept into the president's theater box and shot him in the head. Then he leaped down onto the stage and escaped. Federal agents caught up to Booth in Virginia twelve days later. Booth was shot and killed while trying to flee.

After he was shot,

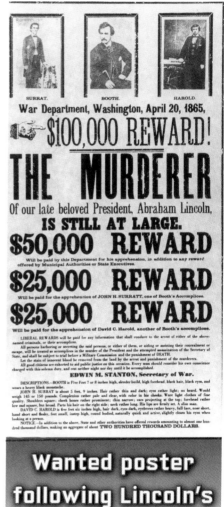

Wanted poster following Lincoln's assassination

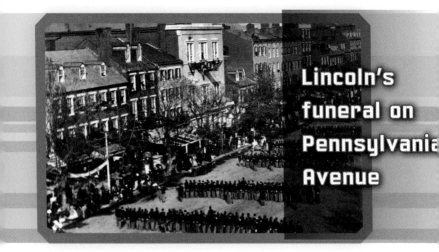

Lincoln's funeral on Pennsylvania Avenue

Lincoln was taken to the Petersen House across the street from the theater. But the army surgeon who examined his wound knew at once that it was fatal. Lincoln had already fallen into a coma. He never woke up, and died nine hours later. His body was buried in Oak Ridge Cemetery in Springfield, Illinois.

Although he only outlived the war by days, Lincoln did see the success of his presidency. He had steered the country through battle, and had reunited the warring states. It was a major accomplishment. The first task of the president is to preserve the country and its government, and he had done that despite many obstacles. Lincoln ended the Gettysburg Address by stating,

We here highly resolve that these dead shall not have died in vain—that this nation, under God, shall have a new birth of freedom—and that government of the people, by the people, for the people, shall not perish from the earth.

Lincoln's firm leadership helped guide the country through the Civil War, and allowed the United States to survive. Without his guidance, the country might have collapsed, and the new freedom he had fought for might never have come to be.

Lincoln Memorial in Washington, D.C.

FREDERICK DOUGLASS

FREDERICK DOUGLASS was the best-known African American in the United States at the time of the Civil War. A former slave, he was a brilliant writer and a powerful speaker who championed freedom for everyone.

THE POWER OF WORDS

FREDERICK AUGUSTUS WASHINGTON BAILEY WAS BORN IN February 1818, nine years after Abraham Lincoln was born. Like Lincoln, he was born in a small cabin. But the Lincolns owned their log cabin. Frederick's family did not. Their home was a slave cabin. His mother was a slave on the Holme Hill Farm, near Easton in eastern Maryland. Like many slaves at that time, Frederick never knew his father. He did not know his mother, Harriet Bailey, very well, either—he was taken from her when he was only a few weeks old. Frederick's grandparents raised him instead. Slave owners often separated children from their parents. This was to keep slaves from forming strong families and standing up to the slave owners.

When Frederick was six, his grandmother took him to their master's plantation, which was called Wye House. Then she left him there. She never even told him she was going to leave. Frederick was left alone with slaves

Wye House

he did not know. He had to learn to do what he was told, like everyone else on the plantation.

Fortunately for Frederick, he did not stay long on the plantation. When he was eight, his first master, Aaron Anthony, died. Slaves were considered property, and could be inherited like a house or money. Frederick became the property of Anthony's son-in-law, Thomas Auld. Thomas did not need another young slave. But his brother Hugh Auld had requested a houseboy, a young slave who ran simple errands and did basic chores around the house. So Thomas Auld sent Frederick to Baltimore.

Hugh's wife, Sophia, took a liking to the quiet young boy. She taught him the alphabet, which opened a whole new world to Frederick. Hugh Auld told his wife she could not teach the boy any more, because slaves were not supposed to know how to read. That was another way slave owners kept their slaves from standing up to them.

Artist's drawing of Douglass

But Frederick had discovered reading, and was determined

to learn more. He started offering food to neighborhood boys in exchange for help learning to read and write. Boys are always hungry, and many of them were happy to repeat their own school lessons for extra food. When he was twelve or thirteen, Frederick talked one of the boys into selling him a copy of *The Columbian Orator*. This was a popular schoolbook back then. The book fascinated Frederick. He was amazed by what simple words could do and how much they could teach.

BATTLE OF WILLS

Sadly, in 1833 the Aulds had some sort of argument with Thomas, who was still Frederick's master. As punishment, Thomas summoned Frederick back to Wye House. Sophia was sorry to see him go, and Frederick was sorry to leave her. He was even unhappier when he returned to the plantation. He had not realized what an easy life he'd had with the Aulds! The conditions on the plantation were terrible! Most of the slaves had only rags to wear and lived in filthy huts. They had barely enough food to survive, and were treated like animals. Actually, the master's dogs were better fed and more pampered.

Frederick was better educated than most of his

fellow slaves. That education made him more confident. Unfortunately, that meant he did not obey orders
as quickly. It also meant he had a harder time dis-
guising his disgust at their living conditions. Thomas
Auld quickly realized that Frederick did not behave
like a proper slave. Thomas knew he had to change
Frederick's attitude. He had to break the young man
of his spirit. He sent Frederick to a neighboring farmer
named Edward Covey. Covey was a hard man. He was
known as a slave breaker, someone who could whip
slaves into shape the same way animal trainers could
tame stubborn dogs.

Covey and Frederick fought for six months. Both
were stubborn men. Frederick was young and bright
and hopeful. Covey was old and bitter and mean. For a
time, Covey won. Frederick later wrote:

Mr. Covey succeeded in breaking me. I was
broken in body, soul, and spirit. My natural elasticity was crushed, my intel-
lect languished, the disposition to read
departed, the cheerful spark that lin-
gered about my eye died; the dark night
of slavery closed in upon me; and behold a
man transformed into a brute!

But Frederick was too stubborn to stay beaten for long. And the more Covey hurt him, the more he resisted. In the end, Covey backed down. Frederick had won. More importantly, he had learned a valuable lesson: No man could truly own him. Even though he was technically a slave, Frederick was free.

But being free in his mind was not enough. Frederick resolved to escape. After Covey, he was sent to work for a man named Freeland. While he was there, Frederick taught some of the other slaves how to read and write. The other slaves looked up to Frederick. He became close friends with four in particular. Together they planned to escape by traveling up the Chesapeake Bay to Baltimore. But somehow Freeman learned of the plan. Frederick and the others were arrested and thrown in jail.

Hugh Auld came to Frederick's rescue. He paid to have Frederick released, and got him a job in the ship-yards. But some of the men there did not like having a slave among them. They felt Frederick was trying to steal their jobs. A band of carpenters ganged up on Frederick and beat him severely. And there was nothing Frederick could do about it. As a slave, he had no rights.

When Hugh and Sophia learned about the beating,

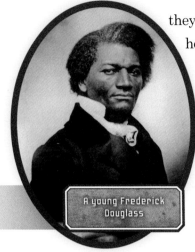

A young Frederick Douglass

they took Frederick into their home again. Hugh found Frederick a job with a different shipbuilder who looked out for the young slave. Frederick liked this new job. He learned how to caulk ships, and he even earned money for his work! The Aulds let him keep some of the money for himself. That was almost unheard of. Working and earning money gave Frederick even more confidence. He knew that he had to be truly free.

In September 1838, Frederick made another attempt to escape. He managed to obtain the papers of a free black sailor, which allowed him to travel. Disguised as that sailor, Frederick said good-bye to Baltimore, the Aulds, and slavery, and boarded a train to Havre de Grace, Maryland. He was twenty years old.

A FREE MAN

It took almost twenty-four hours to get from Baltimore to New York. Frederick had to switch from the train to a ferry to cross the Susquehanna River. Then he took another train to Wilmington, Delaware. From there he boarded a steamboat to Philadelphia, Pennsylvania. Finally he took a train from Philadelphia to New York. But Frederick didn't mind. After so many years, he was finally free of his masters, even the kindly Hugh and Sophia Auld. New York did not allow slavery. Here Frederick could truly be his own man.

Frederick was not alone, either. That same year, he had met a young woman named Anna Murray. Anna was black, but she was a free woman. She lived in Baltimore, and she and Frederick had liked each other immediately. Once Frederick had made it to New York safely, Anna joined him. They married soon after.

Unfortunately, just fleeing Maryland did not make Frederick safe. New York did not allow slavery, but it had no control over the laws of other states. Slavery was legal in Maryland, which meant by law that Frederick was Thomas Auld's property.

Anna Douglass

Auld could offer a reward for Frederick's return. If someone in New York recognized Frederick, they could capture him and take him back. Hunting escaped slaves was a very profitable business. And it was completely legal, because the Fugitive Slave Act of 1850 allowed runaway slaves to be taken back to their home states, even if they were caught in states where slavery was illegal.

Frederick was lucky enough to meet a man named David Ruggles soon after he arrived in New York. Ruggles was the secretary of the New York Vigilance Committee. The committee was a group of private citizens who opposed slavery and helped runaway slaves find new homes and new lives. Ruggles took in Frederick and arranged for Frederick and Anna to be married. He suggested that New York might not be the safest place for them. Too many people came to the city. Sooner or later, someone would see Frederick and recognize him from the wanted posters Thomas Auld was sure to have issued.

Ruggles thought that a smaller town would be a better place for the newlyweds to settle. He helped them arrange passage to the port town of New Bedford, Massachusetts.

A NEW NAME

New Bedford was known as "the Whaling City" because it was one of the most important whaling ports in the world. People there were surprisingly friendly to Frederick and Anna. No one seemed to care that they were black, or worry that they might be escaped slaves. Mr. and Mrs. Nathan Johnson took the young couple under their wings and helped them get settled. It was Mr. Johnson who suggested that Frederick change his last name. Slaves usually took the last name of their first master. Frederick could now choose his own name, his name as a free man. He selected "Douglass" after the character in Sir Walter Scott's poem "The Lady of the Lake." From then on, he was known as Frederick Douglass.

Douglass was happy in New Bedford. There were still some prejudices, and he was unable to find work

Rosetta Douglass

Lewis Douglass

as a ship caulker, but he did get plenty of work as a laborer. It was hard work, but honest, and he got to keep all of the money he earned. He and Anna joined the local black church and made friends with many of their neighbors. Douglass also attended abolition-ist meetings. The abolitionists believed in eliminating slavery once and for all.

SPEAKING OUT

One of the leading abolitionists was a man named William Lloyd Garrison. Garrison was a well-known and eloquent speaker. He and Isaac Knapp also pub-lished a weekly journal called the *Liberator*. Douglass subscribed to the paper and read each issue eagerly. He was excited to see people talking about slavery and how horrible it was. It gave him a sense of belonging, and showed him that many people agreed that slavery was wrong.

During the abolitionist meet-ings, slaves often spoke of their own experiences. At one meeting in October 1841, Douglass was

William Lloyd Garrison

asked to speak. He had never talked about his experiences before, and he had never spoken to a large group, but he managed to tell his story. Afterward, several people told him how moved they had been. One of those people was William Lloyd Garrison.

Garrison was actually so impressed that he wrote about Douglass in the *Liberator*. The Massachusetts Anti-Slavery Society had also been impressed. They invited Douglass to become a public speaker for their organization. He had never considered public speaking before, but discovered that he enjoyed it. And he was good at it. Douglass gave his first speech at the society's annual convention in Nantucket that November.

Soon Douglass was speaking all across the eastern and midwestern United States. He also began collecting his speeches and shaping them into a book about his life as a slave. *Narrative of the Life of Frederick Douglass, An American Slave* was published in 1845. Many people refused to believe a black man could write so eloquently, but the book became an immediate bestseller.

Douglass had been careful not to reveal details that could endanger other escaped slaves. He did not talk about how he had escaped, for example. He only revealed those details years later. He also never used real names in his books. But it would not have been that hard for someone to figure out who his masters had been back in Maryland. And because the book was so popular, Douglass's name and picture were everywhere. He worried that his former masters would come after him or that people would capture him for the reward. Fortunately Douglass's friends had the answer. On August 16, 1845, Douglass and Anna set sail for Liverpool, England.

Charles Douglass

Frederick Douglass, Jr.

TIME ABROAD

The Douglasses spent the next two years overseas. They traveled around the United Kingdom. Douglass spoke in churches and chapels across the country. People flocked to his lectures. There were still people who looked down upon Douglass for the color of his skin. But no one in the United Kingdom had a problem with his past as a slave. And the Fugitive Slave Acts of the United States did not extend to Great Britain.

Douglass made many new friends in England. In late 1846 they proved just how much they liked and respected this young man from Maryland. His friends united to purchase his freedom from his former owner for one hundred and fifty pounds. On December 5, 1846, Frederick Douglass legally became a free man. Now he no longer had to worry about slave hunters dragging him back to the plantation.

A NORTHERN STAR

In 1847 the Douglasses returned to the United States and settled in Rochester, New York. The following year Douglass began a new venture. He started his own newspaper. The *North Star* was "devoted to the cause of liberty and progress," Douglass announced in his second book, *My Bondage and My Freedom.*

After three years, Douglass merged his *North Star* with Gerrit Smith's *Liberty Party Paper* to create *Frederick Douglass' Paper.* They continued to publish the paper until 1860. Douglass also published *Frederick Douglass' Weekly, Douglass' Monthly,* and *New National Era.* Each paper carried his message of freedom for all, and urged the abolishment of slavery.

Douglass's belief in freedom did not end with black men. He believed women should have equal rights as well. In 1848 he participated in the first women's rights convention in Seneca Falls, New York. He was the only African American there. He also spoke frequently about education and how important it was for everyone. Learning to read and write had saved him from slavery. Douglass was sure it could save countless others. But African American children were not allowed to attend white schools. And the schools available for African Americans were smaller and cruder and had inferior teachers and materials. He urged people to correct this injustice. He even demanded that the courts force schools to allow all children to attend, no matter their race.

Writing and speaking were not the only ways

Douglass fought to right wrongs. The Underground Railroad was a loose organization of men and women who helped smuggle slaves out of the proslavery states and helped them establish new lives as free men and women. Douglass became a stationmaster for the Underground Railroad. That meant he was responsible for many of the slaves passing through his area. Anyone caught helping an escaped slave faced severe punishment. But Douglass believed aiding others was well worth the risk.

OFF TO WAR

When the Civil War began, many free black men wanted to enlist. They were willing to fight to preserve their freedom and that of their children. Douglass felt that way as well. He became a recruiter for the 54th Massachusetts Regiment, which was the first black unit in the Union army. His eldest son, Frederick Douglass, Jr., also helped recruit, and his other son, Lewis, fought in the 54th. More than one hundred and eighty

Sergeant Henry F. Steward of the 54th Massachusetts Regiment

thousand African Americans fought in the Union army. It is entirely possible that the Union would have lost the war without their help.

Unfortunately, at the start of the war, many of the white soldiers behaved horribly toward the African American recruits. Members of African American units were also paid far less than their white counterparts, and received far worse equipment, weapons, and rations. The African American soldiers faced an additional problem as well. Most soldiers could expect to be ransomed back to their army if they were captured. But the Confederate army considered any African American soldier to be an escaped slave. Instead of treating them

54th Massachusetts Regiment memorial in Boston

well, the Confederates either executed any African American prisoners or sold them back into slavery.

When Douglass saw how other soldiers treated the members of the 54th, he could not keep quiet. Most people would have complained to the local army officers. But Douglass knew that the best way to get anything done was to go to the very top. So in July 1863 he went to speak to the president. Fortunately, Douglass was a famous speaker, writer, and abolitionist. Lincoln was only too happy to meet with him and discuss the situation. Together they tried to find ways to make sure the 54th Regiment was treated the same as any other army unit. Others helped as well, including Clara Barton, who ministered to wounded soldiers throughout the Union army but gave the 54th as much attention as possible.

Douglass also helped Lincoln find ways to get liberated slaves safely out of the South and into the Union states. The two men had many things in common. Both had started off poor and humble. Both had become famous speakers and influential leaders. And both

Clara Barton

wanted what was fair for everyone. "In his company," Douglass wrote, "I was never in any way reminded of my humble origin, or of my unpopular color." He and Lincoln became good friends, and he became one of the president's most trusted advisors.

Douglass was in Rochester when Lincoln died. He was devastated by the news. The country had lost its leader, but he had also lost his good friend.

FREDERICK DOUGLASS AND GEORGE MCCLELLAN

Despite their friendship and years of working together, Douglass almost didn't support Lincoln for reelection! Douglass knew his friend was torn between abolishing slavery and keeping the peace. He felt Lincoln sometimes put off doing the right thing because it could upset too many people. Douglass had been hoping to find and support a presidential candidate with stronger antislavery convictions. In September 1864, he changed his mind, however, and encouraged everyone to rally to Lincoln's banner. One reason Douglass chose to support Lincoln again was the Democratic Party's decision to nominate General George B. McClellan for president. As Douglass wrote: "When we were thus asked to exchange Abraham Lincoln for McClellan—a successful Union president for an unsuccessful Union general . . . I thought with Mr. Lincoln, that it was not wise to 'swap horses while crossing a stream.'"

MORE GOOD WORK

Though his friend Lincoln died immediately after the war, Douglass lived on. And he continued to work toward freedom and equality for everyone. After their house in Rochester burned down in 1872, the Douglasses moved to Washington, D.C. It was the perfect place for Douglass. His activities during the Civil War had made him more famous than ever. And his friendship with Lincoln had thrust him into the realm of politics and big business.

Douglass was made president of the newly formed Freedman's Savings Bank in 1874. In 1877 he was appointed U.S. marshal for the District of Columbia. In 1881 he was made recorder of deeds for the District of Columbia. He served as the consul general to Haiti from 1888 to 1891.

Douglass devoted a great deal of his time to the Equal Rights Party, lobbying for women and African Americans to be allowed to vote. And in 1868 he supported former Union general Ulysses S. Grant's bid for president. Four years later, Douglass himself was nominated for vice president on Victoria Woodhull's Equal Rights Party ticket. He may have felt the position was premature, however. Whatever the reason,

FREDERICK DOUGLASS'S THOUGHTS ON LINCOLN

Frederick Douglass and Abraham Lincoln had grown to be close friends during the Civil War. Years later, at the unveiling of the Freedmen's Memorial in Lincoln Park in Washington, D.C., Frederick said:

"Though high in position, the humblest could approach him and feel at home in his presence. Though deep, he was transparent; though strong, he was gentle; though decided and pronounced in his convictions, he was tolerant towards those who differed from him, and patient under reproaches."

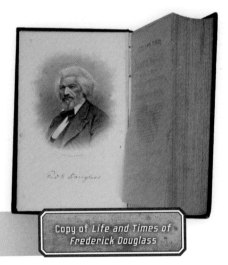

Copy of *Life and Times of Frederick Douglass*

Douglass never acknowledged the nomination or campaigned for himself or Woodhull.

Douglass had written his second autobiography, *My Bondage and My Freedom*, in 1855. In 1881 he published his third and final book, *Life and Times of Frederick Douglass*. This third book openly revealed details about his escape from slavery. There was no longer any reason to hide such information.

Anna Douglass died on August 4, 1882. Two years later, Douglass married his secretary, Helen Pitts. Helen was an outspoken editor and lecturer in her own right. She was a strong supporter of the women's rights movement. She was also white. Many people frowned upon the marriage, but the two were well matched. They spent much of 1886 and 1887 traveling to Europe, Britain, and the Mediterranean.

Helen Pitts Douglass

In 1892, Douglass helped construct a housing complex in Fells Point in Baltimore. It was designed to provide affordable housing for African Americans until they could acquire jobs and find new homes of their own. The complex was later named Douglass Place.

A SWIFT END

On February 20, 1895, Douglass was at a meeting for

Douglass's house in Washington, D.C.

the National Council of Women. He was not speaking at the meeting, but was invited up onto the platform anyway. The attendees gave him a standing ovation. Douglass returned home afterward. He suffered a massive heart attack or a major stroke soon after. It was a swift and fatal blow. He was buried in Mount Hope Cemetery in his former hometown of Rochester, New York.

In one of his last speeches, delivered on March 31, 1888, to the International Council of Women, Frederick Douglass had said:

Whatever the future may have in store for us, one thing is certain—this new revolution in human thought will never go backward. When a great truth once gets abroad in the world, no power on earth can imprison it, or prescribe its limits, or suppress it. It is bound to go on till it becomes the thought of the world.

For many, Frederick Douglass helped spread those truths. His voice was one of the loudest, clearest, and finest speaking out against slavery. And his words helped create that great truth of freedom.

Statue of Douglass in Rochester, New York

CLARA BARTON

CLARA BARTON was a teacher and nurse. She provided medical care for the men fighting in the Civil War. After the war, she founded the American Red Cross.

EARLY TRAINING

CLARISSA "CLARA" HARLOWE BARTON WAS BORN ON December 25, 1821, in Oxford, Massachusetts. She was the youngest of five children. Her parents were both abolitionists. Her father, Captain Stephen Barton, was

a successful farmer and horse breeder. He was also the captain of the local militia. He told his children stories about the battles he had experienced. Clara Barton and the others learned geography and military

Childhood home in Oxford, Massachusetts

tactics from those stories. She also learned the importance of supplies and medical care for soldiers. The old saying "an army travels on its stomach" is very true. It means that without supplies an army will be too weak to fight, so it's important to make sure the army has enough food and other supplies.

The Bartons believed in being prepared, and taught their children the same principle. The children learned horseback riding and other important lessons. Their mother taught them at home instead of sending them

The Barton family moved to this house when Clara Barton was nine.

to school. Barton was the baby of the family, and her big brothers and big sisters helped with her education: Dorothy taught her spelling, Stephen taught her arithmetic, Sally taught her geography, and David taught her athletics. Barton was an excellent student, but she enjoyed the outdoor activities as much as studying.

When Barton was eleven, she had a chance to practice the medical aid she'd learned. Her brother David broke his leg, and Barton helped tend to him. Back then people didn't know as much about how to heal injuries, and David's leg did not heal properly. He was sick for three years as a result. Barton stayed at his side the whole time. She even learned how to administer all of his medicines.

David Barton

GETTING AHEAD

Barton grew into a clever and accomplished young woman. But she was painfully shy. Then, when she was sixteen, her parents insisted that becoming a teacher would be the perfect way for Barton to gain more confidence and become more comfortable speaking to others.

In those days, teachers did not require a special degree. They just had to have a good education. That wasn't a problem for Barton! She had always been an excellent student.

The other thing a teacher needed was a schoolhouse. Fortunately, good teachers were in high demand. Barton was soon offered a job teaching at a one-room schoolhouse in Massachusetts District 9, in Worcester County. Back then, schools rarely had more than one big room. The students all sat together, and the teacher gave each student assignments based upon his or her ability.

One big problem for most teachers was maintaining discipline. Students only went to school when they could be spared from their chores. Most schools were cancelled during planting season or harvest time because all the students were busy working. That meant the students didn't get into a regular routine throughout the year. It also meant they didn't listen to their teachers as well. After all, they only saw their teachers for a few months. And most teachers were young women. The older boys were often bigger than their teachers!

Barton had a rare ability to keep her students interested. She told them stories, just like her father had with her. She also organized her classes carefully. Barton liked to write out detailed lesson plans, working out in advance what she would teach each day.

After teaching in District 9 for six years, Barton decided to start her own school in North Oxford. That made it easier for her to teach the way she wanted. And her teaching methods got results.

FURTHER EDUCATION

Eventually Barton decided that she needed to learn even more if she wanted to be able to teach better. In 1850 she enrolled in the Clinton Liberal Institute in Clinton, New York. Barton took language and writing courses there. She studied at the institute for one year. There were no formal degrees, so people studied only as long as they wanted. The institute catered primarily to female teachers.

Barton in 1850

After Barton completed her studies, her friends Charles and Mary Norton invited her to visit with their family in Hightstown, New Jersey. Barton liked the area, and got a job teaching in nearby Cedarville and then in Bordentown. She was surprised to discover there were no free schools in New Jersey. Back in Massachusetts, the state ran several schools that any child could attend for free. In New Jersey, the only schools were private schools that parents had to pay for their children to attend. Most parents couldn't afford to send their children to private schools. That meant most children in New Jersey could not get an education.

Barton decided that was unacceptable. So she started her own free school. It wasn't necessary to have a license or fill out any forms. She just needed a schoolhouse and some students. Barton went around

Bordentown and spread the word about her new school. A lot of parents were nervous about sending their children to a new school with a teacher no one knew. To convince them, Barton offered to teach the first six months for free!

On the first day of class, six students showed up. Barton had hoped for more, but she was happy anyone came at all.

Barton took her teaching as seriously as ever. And her new students responded as well as her old students in Massachusetts had. Soon word got out about the new public school and its wonderful teacher. By the end of the year, Barton had more than two hundred students!

Barton's schoolhouse in Bordentown, New Jersey

The people of Bordentown were extremely impressed. And they loved the idea of having a public school. They spent four thousand dollars to build a nice new school building big enough to accommodate all the children. They also hired more teachers so each student could get more attention. Barton was thrilled—until she found out that she would not be the one running the school. Instead, the town hired a man as the principal of Schoolhouse Number One. And they paid him twice as much as she had been making!

Annoyed and insulted, Barton resigned and left New Jersey. She needed a fresh start somewhere. She chose Washington, D.C.

EARLY EQUALITY

Barton was furious that a man would be offered more than her for the same job. As she wrote later:

"I may sometimes be willing to teach for nothing, but if paid at all, I shall never do a man's work for less than a man's pay."

OFFICE WORK

In 1854 Barton moved to Washington, D.C. She decided not to go back to teaching. That meant she needed a new job. Fortunately, she was well educated and organized.

The den in Barton's Washington, D.C. home

These were attractive qualities and made her a good choice for lots of jobs. She finally took a position as a clerk at the U.S. Patent Office. The Patent Office handled patents, which people requested to protect their inventions and ideas so no one could steal them. Filing a patent was a long and complicated process, and it required patience and attention to detail. Barton was the first female clerk in the office. She was also making as much as the male clerks, which was rare. Most women made far less than men doing the same job.

Barton enjoyed working in the Patent Office. It was quiet and organized. But there was a lot of work to be done. And some of her male coworkers started to pester her. They were annoyed that a woman was doing the same work and earning the same salary. Then, when James Buchanan won the presidential election of 1856, his administration changed the rules for hiring women in government positions. Barton found herself out of a job.

The government's policies toward women changed slightly when Lincoln became president in 1860, and Barton received an invitation to return to the Patent Office, but not as a full-time clerk. Instead, they asked her to work as a temporary copyist. She would earn eight cents per one hundred words, which was less than she had made before. At first Barton did not want to accept. But Senator Henry Wilson of Massachusetts offered to help her fight for equal pay. Barton decided to take the job in order to pave the way for others.

OLD WOUNDED FRIENDS

On April 19, 1861, troops from the 6th Regiment Massachusetts Volunteer Militia arrived in Washington. Confederate sympathizers had attacked them when they'd reached Baltimore, and they were ragged, wounded, and confused. Barton and her sister Sally Vassall went to the train station to meet them and see how they could help. They had grown up with many of these men. Barton was horrified to learn that the city did not have any place to put the wounded soldiers, or any way to care for them. Most of

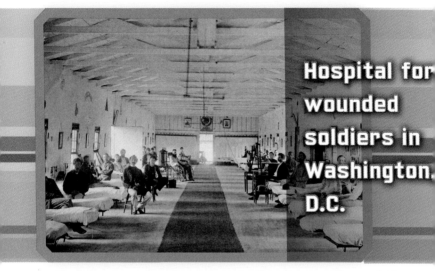

Hospital for wounded soldiers in Washington, D.C.

their baggage had been lost during the scuffle, and the men had no clothing or supplies.

Barton took charge at once. She brought the more heavily wounded men to her sister's house and found accommodations for the others. She went around to local merchants and convinced them to donate food, clothing, and supplies to outfit the men. It was not easy, and Barton was kept busy running from place to place. But she thrived on the chance to be useful to others. And these men clearly needed her help.

Soon, more troops reached Washington. When volunteer soldiers from New York and New Jersey arrived, she recognized many of her former students. They were thrilled to see Miss Barton again, and naturally turned to her for advice and direction. And Barton was only too happy to provide it. She began visiting the men in their camps around the city.

Barton knew that she couldn't ask the merchants in Washington to supply things for everyone. Fortunately, she had friends in other states as well. She wrote to people in Massachusetts, New York, and New Jersey. Many of them agreed to help. They sent what they could. The soldiers wrote home and asked for help as well. They all instructed their family and friends to send things to Miss Barton. Soon she was receiving lots of donations for "her boys." Without even meaning to, she had established a network of support and supply for the Union army.

The first American Red Cross emergency case

FULL-TIME AID

As the Civil War began in earnest, Barton reached a decision. She decided she could not take a salary from the government when most of its money was needed to support the war. Besides, she had something more important to do than file patents!

Barton resigned from the Patent Office. She devoted herself full-time to aiding the war any way she could. At first that meant using her contacts and her growing network to obtain supplies. But the First Battle of Bull Run in July 1861 changed that. The Union army was badly beaten, and many of the men were hurt. The most important thing now was not getting supplies but

Photo taken shortly after the Battle of Bull Run

BARTON'S DEDICATION

Barton was strong willed and determined. As she had told the women of the Worcester Ladies' Relief Committee when asking them to send supplies:

"I will remain here while anyone remains. I may be compelled to face danger, but never fear it, and while our soldiers can stand and fight, I can stand and feed and nurse them."

ministering to the wounded. Barton's old experience with her brother came back to her. She volunteered at once to help nurse soldiers on the battlefield.

Women were not allowed on the battlefield. It was considered an inappropriate place for them, and far too dangerous. But Barton had grown up handling herself as well as any boy. And she would not be stopped from helping. General William Hammond agreed to let Barton ride in the army ambulances. That way she could help comfort and tend to soldiers once they had been retrieved from the battlefield. It was a first step, but it was not enough for her. Barton needed to nurse the wounded where they lay if they were to have any chance of recovery.

Barton petitioned the government. Her prior experience as a teacher and a government clerk showed them that she was organized, thorough, and careful. That helped convince them that she could handle the situation. So did her friendship with the soldiers from her old homes, and the supply network she had established. In August 1862 she was granted permission to travel behind the lines and work on the battlefields themselves.

In order to help, Barton knew she had to be there when the battles took place. She also resolved to bring her own supplies to the war so she would not have to rely upon whatever the army could offer. She obtained a quartermaster's pass (which she needed in order to pass through military lines) and six wagons, and found teamsters to drive them. Then she began to travel with the army itself. The soldiers who knew

Monument at the Antietam National Battlefield about Clara Barton

her were thrilled. When she first reached Antietam and Fredericksburg, the 21st Infantry Regiment Massachusetts held a dress parade in her honor and made her an official daughter of the regiment. Other Union army units soon learned to recognize and respect Barton. One thing they all liked about her was that she considered herself one of them right from the start. She ate what they ate and went where they went. It was dangerous, but Barton was determined to share the danger faced by these young men, who were risking their lives for their country.

THE ANGEL IN MOTION

At first many of the army officials resented Barton's presence. She was a distraction, and someone they thought they needed to protect. She was also a civilian interfering in military matters.

Over time, however, they learned their mistake. Barton was no timid woman cowering on the sidelines. She was strong and tough and determined. She had taught herself nursing all over again so she could care for the wounded. And she was not afraid to tend to them right there during a battle. At one point during the Battle of Antietam, Barton knelt to help a

Illustration of Barton tending to a wounded soldier

wounded soldier. While she offered him a drink, a bullet whizzed past her, so close it nicked her sleeve. She noticed the bullet hole, and only then realized that the same bullet had just killed the man she was tending. A few inches to the side and it would have killed her as well. But Barton did not let that thought stop her. Instead she rose and moved to the next man in need, and then the one after him.

The Union officers grew to respect and admire Barton's bravery and determination. Her strong will and careful organization saved many lives throughout the war, and her willingness to nurse men even while battles raged around her saved many more. The men began referring to Barton as the "Angel of the Battlefield," and soon the officers called her by that title as well.

In 1864 President Lincoln made Barton's role official. He named her superintendent of Union nurses and gave her full authority to gather and administer

Lincoln with Union soldiers at Antietam

supplies and direct assistants wherever she needed—including on the battlefield. She was also charged with establishing and organizing hospitals for the army, wherever she deemed them necessary.

Barton was pleased. Now no one could argue that she had a right to be there, in the thick of it all, helping.

She did more than just direct, of course. Time and again Barton extended herself to help the wounded, both on and off the battlefield. More than once she exhausted herself in the process. After Antietam, she had to be taken back to Washington in the back of a wagon. She had collapsed from lack of sleep and the start of typhoid fever. But as soon as she had recovered, Barton was back on the battlefield, wearing her familiar bonnet, red bow, and dark skirt.

Union casualties

FINDING THE MISSING

The Civil War ended in 1865, but Barton knew her work was not yet over. There were still soldiers who needed to be healed. And, in the chaos of the war, many others had gone missing. What had happened to these courageous young men? Barton was determined to find out.

She was not the only one interested. Shortly before his death, President Lincoln personally charged her with searching for missing Union soldiers. Barton hoped to find these men and return them to their loved ones. For those who had died unnoticed, she wanted their deaths to be acknowledged and mourned.

Her efforts got significant help when a young soldier arrived at her doorstep one day. His name was Dorence Atwater. He had been one of many held in a prisoner-of-war camp in Andersonville, Georgia. Many of the men there had been tortured, and most had died. Atwater had secretly copied the names of the dead, and smuggled the list out when he was released after the war. He had heard of Clara Barton's campaign, and knew she was the right person to help him release those names. Working together, Barton and Atwater published the Atwater List. More than thirteen thousand missing Union soldiers were found and buried with full honors thanks to their efforts. It took forty-two carvers to craft all the headstones once they were allowed to bury the newly identified remains.

Barton's efforts found many other Union soldiers.

Barton nursing hospitalized army men

Some of them had been killed, like those in Andersonville, but others were still alive. All told, she helped locate close to twenty-two thousand missing men.

TRAVEL AND TREATIES

After the war, many people wanted to hear about Barton's experiences on the battlefield. She began traveling the lecture circuit. She met Susan B. Anthony, one of the leading figures in the fight for women's rights, and the two women began a long friendship. Barton also met Frederick Douglass, who had helped found the 54th Regiment out of Massachusetts. The 54th had been the first regiment of black soldiers, and Barton had struggled to make sure they had proper equipment, supplies, and care when many of their fellow sol-

Susan B. Anthony

diers and commanding officers slighted them. She was delighted to make Frederick Douglass's acquaintance in these quieter times, and their encounter convinced her to become an activist for black civil rights as well. Barton also met famous authors, like Ralph Waldo Emerson and Mark Twain.

By 1868 she had delivered more than two hundred lectures!

By 1869 Barton had exhausted herself again. Her doctors advised her to stop working for a while. They suggested she travel. Barton decided that was a good idea, and so she traveled to Switzerland. While there, she learned about the Treaty of Geneva. It guaranteed basic rights and humane treatment to soldiers and prisoners of war in any of the countries that had signed it. The treaty also established the Red Cross, an organization that ministered the wounded and made sure no one was mistreated under the terms of the treaty. She even saw the Red Cross in action when she volunteered her aid during the Franco-Prussian War in 1870.

Barton was fascinated. She had spent the Civil War trying to make sure Union soldiers received similar care! What if she could bring the Red Cross to the United States as well?

She began work on this project as soon as she returned to the United

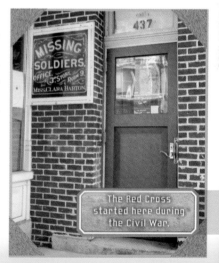

The Red Cross started here during the Civil War.

Clara Barton
postage stamp

States in 1873. She lobbied for the country to sign the treaty and create its own branch of the Red Cross. Barton was not convinced that the existing treaty was broad enough, however. She wanted the Red Cross to lend aid during any national disaster, not just war.

It was not an easy proposition. Most of the country believed they would never face a crisis like the Civil War again. But Barton knew it was better to be prepared. She had moved to Dansville, New York, in 1876, and on May 21, 1881, she established the first chapter of the American Red Cross there. The following year, President James Garfield agreed to her proposal. He signed the treaty, and the United States became part of the International Red Cross. Barton remained president of the American Red Cross, and ran the organization for the next twenty-two years. It provided aid during many natural disasters, including the floods of the Mississippi and Ohio rivers in 1882 and 1884, the famine in Texas in 1886, the yellow fever epidemic in Florida in 1887, and a similar epidemic in Illinois in 1889.

LEAVING QUIETLY

Barton resigned as president of the American Red Cross in 1904. She spent the next eight years quietly in Glen Echo, Maryland. She rode horses frequently, and enjoyed speaking with people, visiting, and keeping an eye on current events.

In the spring of 1912, Barton caught a cold. She was ninety-one at the time, and the minor illness overwhelmed her. She died on April 12, 1912. She was the most decorated woman in America, and had been awarded the Iron Cross, the Cross of Imperial Russia, and the International Red Cross Medal.

Barton's hard work and determination improved the lives of many, and her work with the American Red Cross created an organization that would improve people's lives for years to come.

Barton writing at her desk

GEORGE McCLELLAN

GEORGE McCLELLAN was a general of the Union army during the Civil War. Though not always successful in battle, he was largely responsible for building, organizing, and training the military.

HIGH EXPECTATIONS

GEORGE BRINTON MCCLELLAN WAS BORN IN PHILADELPHIA on December 3, 1826. His grandfather, Samuel McClellan, had been a general in the Revolutionary War. His father, George, was a renowned doctor and the founder of the Jefferson Medical College. His mother, Elizabeth Steinmetz Brinton McClellan, came from a successful and wealthy family herself. George was the third of five children. His family was wealthy and well respected. Everyone expected great things from all five children, especially from George and his brothers, John and Arthur.

As a boy, McClellan received tutoring from a Harvard graduate named Sears Cook Walker. Then he attended the University of Pennsylvania Preparatory School. In 1840 he enrolled at the University of Pennsylvania itself. At that time, it was rare for people to go to college. Most colleges only offered three degrees: a student could prepare to become a doctor, a

George McClellan (left) with his father and brother, Arthur

lawyer, or a priest. McClellan studied law. The idea of being a lawyer did not appeal to him, however. He had only gone to college to please his family.

McClellan was not entirely sure what he did want to do. But he was interested in the military. He decided to apply to West Point. West Point was the country's most prestigious military academy. It had very strict entrance requirements. Everyone who graduated from West Point became an officer in the U.S. Army.

Normally, you had to be sixteen years old to enter West Point. McClellan was only fifteen and seven months when he decided to go. Fortunately for him, his father was a powerful man. Dr. McClellan wrote a letter to President John Tyler on his son's behalf. The president and McClellan's father both wrote letters asking West Point to overlook McClellan's age. The academy decided to accept him based on his "mental ability and fine physique."

In June 1842 McClellan began studying at West Point. He wrote to his older sister,

John
Tyler

Frederica, frequently. Classes at West Point were very tough. The academy expected the best from all its cadets. McClellan was not sure he could handle the pressure or the work. But he was smart and friendly and determined to succeed. He made friends and learned the routines of the academy. The structure and discipline of

A young George McClellan

West Point worked well for McClellan. He became an excellent student. When he graduated in 1846, he was second in his class out of fifty-nine remaining cadets. There had been 164 cadets originally.

Because he had placed so highly, McClellan was able to request where he wanted to go in the army. He chose to serve as an engineer, which meant he would deal with surveying and reconnaissance. He was made a brevet second lieutenant in his company and was told to prepare to travel to Mexico. Mexico and the United States were quarreling over who owned Texas, and it looked likely that the argument would lead to war.

OFF TO MEXICO

McClellan and his company arrived in Brazos de Santiago, Mexico, in late September 1846. They then marched to the city of Tampico, then to Veracruz, and finally to Mexico City. McClellan was eager to display the skills he had learned at West Point. Unfortunately, the long march and the heat weakened him. He came down with malaria and dysentery, and spent almost a month in the hospital.

Though the army had no trouble with Tampico, the faced stiff resistance at Veracruz and beyond. McClellan served bravely in each of the battles. His tactics and his ability to make decisions impressed his superiors. They promoted him to first lieutenant, and then to captain.

During the Mexican-American War, McClellan experienced combat firsthand. He also discovered the difference between learning about a war and fighting one. He saw how undisciplined most of the volunteer soldiers were compared to West Point–trained men. McClellan served under Lieutenant General Winfield Scott and learned a great deal from the man. Scott maintained strict discipline among his men but also made sure they had everything they needed.

General Winfield Scott

The Mexican-American War had begun on April 25, 1846. McClellan and his company arrived after the initial battles. The United States won the war on February 2, 1848. Mexico signed the Treaty of Guadalupe Hidalgo and acknowledged that they no longer owned Texas. The United States also got Alta California, Santa Fé de Nuevo México, and all the territory north of the Rio Grande.

McClellan had done well during the war, but he also received some bad news while in Mexico. His father passed away on May 9, 1847, and left the family in debt. McClellan did not make much money as a military officer. He helped his brother James take care of the debts anyway. Family was very important to him.

Mexican Soldiers surrendering their arms to the U.S. Army

BAYONETS AND BEYOND

McClellan was not sure what to do with himself after the Mexican-American War. The United States was not at war, so it did not need combat officers or engineers as much. McClellan returned to West Point, but not as a student. Instead, he became an instructor there at the young age of twenty-two. McClellan soon proved to be an expert at teaching how to use a bayonet. In 1852 he even translated a French manual on the subject. He titled his version *Bayonet Exercise, or School of the Infantry Soldier, in the Use of the Musket in*

Hand-to-Hand Conflicts. The manual quickly became West Point's textbook on the subject.

In 1853 McClellan participated in the Pacific Railroad surveys to select the best route for the transcontinental railroad (a railroad that would cover the entire country). He was responsible for surveying the region from St. Paul, Minnesota, to the Puget Sound in Washington State. Unfortunately, McClellan got himself into trouble on this assignment. For some reason he selected a particular pass without thoroughly examining all of the other options. It was later discovered that three passes were far better than the one he had chosen. When Isaac Stevens, the governor of the Washington Territory, ordered McClellan to turn over his expedition logbooks, McClellan refused.

After he returned home, McClellan began dating Ellen Mary Marcy, the daughter of Captain Randolph B. Marcy. He proposed to Ellen in 1853, but she refused. She was a very popular young woman, and had nine different men ask her to marry them! McClellan was persistent, however. He continued to pursue her, and in 1856 she accepted his proposal. But Ellen's family did not approve, and McClellan was forced to withdraw his proposal.

In 1854 Secretary of War Jefferson Davis ordered McClellan to Santo Domingo to study the local defenses there. McClellan impressed Davis with his sharp mind and keen observations. In March of that year Davis assigned McClellan to the 1st U.S. Cavalry regiment. In 1855 McClellan and two other officers, Major Richard Delafield and Major Alfred Mordecai, went to Europe to observe the Crimean War. It was the first war to use modern technologies, like railroads and telegraphs. The war ended in 1856 and McClellan wrote a thorough report after he

McClellan (right) during the Crimean War

returned to America. He also wrote a manual on cavalry tactics he had seen in the Russian cavalry units. He even designed a new cavalry saddle, modeling it on ones he had seen used by the Hussars of Prussia and Hungary. The army liked McClellan's saddle so much they used the design for the cavalry for many years.

CIVILIAN LIFE

McClellan was becoming tired of being sent on short-term missions. And he was tired of the poor pay the military provided. On January 16, 1857, he resigned his commission. Thanks to his training and experience, McClellan received several job offers right away. He soon signed on as chief engineer of the Illinois Central Railroad. McClellan enjoyed working with the railroad, and he expanded the line toward New Orleans. He soon became a vice president of the company. In 1860 he was offered the position of president of the Ohio and Mississippi Railroad.

McClellan had other reasons to leave the military as well. In October 1859 he began to court Ellen Marcy again. Her parents no longer objected to the match. After all, McClellan had left the army and had a good

George and Ellen
McClellan

job with the railroad. He and Ellen were married in Calvary Church in New York on May 22, 1860.

MILITARY ONCE MORE

In April 1861 the Civil War began. McClellan was living in Ohio and heading the Ohio and Mississippi Railroad at the time. His previous military experience, excellent military reports, and knowledge of the railroads all made the Union army want him back. The Confederate army was also interested in having McClellan on their side, and several of his old friends from West Point approached him about the possibility. McClellan did not believe the federal government should interfere on the matter of slavery, but he did not approve of states seceding from the Union. Even though his former mentor, Jefferson Davis, had been selected as president of the Confederate states, McClellan felt his place was with the United States and their military.

The governors of Ohio, Pennsylvania, and New

York all asked McClellan to lead their state militias. McClellan accepted the offer from Ohio Governor William Dennison Jr., and became a major general of the volunteer militia on April 23. On May 14 he was offered the rank of major general in the regular army. McClellan now reported directly to the Union's general in chief, his old Mexican-American War commander, Winfield Scott. McClellan got to work at once. He established training camps for the men and started organizing his volunteers into a proper fighting force.

McClellan had hoped to keep the Confederacy from claiming control of Kentucky. Since Scott had refused that plan, McClellan concentrated his efforts on western Virginia instead. The eastern portion of that state favored secession, but the western half wanted to remain in the Union. McClellan rallied his new troops and marched. His main concern was reaching western Virginia before rebels burned the Baltimore and Ohio Railroad bridges and blocked them completely.

McClellan led his men through Grafton and fought Robert E. Lee's Confederate forces at the Battle of Philippi. This may have been the first actual land battle of the Civil War. McClellan himself commanded his forces at the Battle of Rich Mountain. They won both combats, even though McClellan hesitated to commit his reserve forces at Rich Mountain. Winning the two battles, and claiming western Virginia for the Union, made McClellan a national hero.

RISING TO THE TOP

On July 21, 1861, the two armies collided at the Battle of Bull Run in Virginia. Brigadier General Irvin McDowell led the Union forces and hoped to sweep through Virginia to the Confederate capital of Richmond. Brigadier General P. G. T. Beauregard stood in his way. Then a second Confederate general,

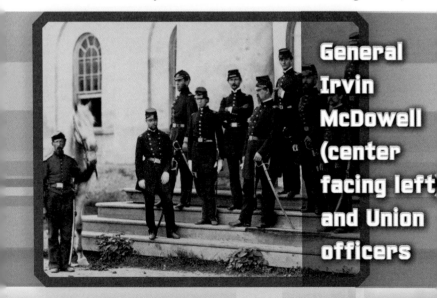

General Irvin McDowell (center facing left) and Union officers

Joseph E. Johnston, arrived with reinforcements. The Union was forced to withdraw. The defeat was a crushing blow to the Union's morale.

President Lincoln blamed McDowell for the loss. McDowell's men had not been well trained or well prepared. They had failed to take control, despite originally having an advantage in numbers. Lincoln removed McDowell from command and put the current Union hero in his place. On July 26, George McClellan became commander of the main Union force, the Military Division of the Potomac.

McClellan reorganized the army units in the area and formed the Army of the Potomac. He was very concerned about proper organization, training, and discipline, and spent the summer and fall of that year preparing his army. The public wanted the soldiers to attack the Confederacy more quickly and end the war as soon as possible. But McClellan knew that an unprepared and disorganized army would not win anything. His preparation took time, but he knew would be worth it in the long run.

One drawback to such lengthy preparation was that it took McClellan away from his family. His daughter, Mary, was born on October 12, 1861, but McClellan did not get to see her very much during her first few years.

On November 1, 1861, Winfield Scott resigned from the military. That meant the Union army no longer had a general in chief. The public still had great faith in McClellan, and Lincoln agreed. He promoted McClellan to general in chief of the Union forces right away. McClellan used his new authority to plan a major offensive for the spring of 1862. His goal was to push through to Richmond and take the city. If the Union could accomplish that, it could end the war. At the same time, McClellan established forty-eight forts around Washington to defend the Union capital from similar attacks. Part of this was because McClellan kept overestimating the Confederacy's forces. He declared a state of emergency in Washington, D.C., on August 8, because he believed the Confederates had over one hundred thousand troops ready to attack. In reality, they had barely thirty-five thousand. A week later, McClellan upped his estimate to one hundred and fifty thousand Confederate soldiers, when they had sixty thousand at most. The Army of the Potomac, meanwhile, numbered more than one hundred and twenty thousand men in September, and more than one hundred and seventy thousand by early December.

If he had realized his advantage, McClellan might have agreed to an earlier attack and won the Civil War after a single year of conflict.

DELAYS AND CONFLICTS

By the beginning of 1862, everyone was impatient for McClellan to attack the Confederacy. On January 12 President Lincoln's cabinet summoned McClellan to the White House and demanded to hear his plans for the war. McClellan explained that he would be transporting the Army of the Potomac to Urbanna, Virginia, by boat. They would then march fifty miles to capture Richmond from behind the Confederate lines. He refused to provide additional details, however.

Lincoln was furious. On January 27 he ordered the Union armies to begin an attack by Washington's Birthday, on February 22. Four days later, he added anoher order—for the Army of the Potomac to attack the Confederates at Manassas Junction and Centreville. McClellan replied with a twenty-two-page letter objecting to the president's plan and detailing his Urbanna plan instead. Lincoln was not happy to be contradicted, but McClellan had shown he was moving, so the president agreed.

When General Johnston withdrew his Confederate troops from Washington and took up a new position below the Rappahannock River, McClellan's Urbanna plan became useless. That had been the very river he had intended to use to move his troops! The press and

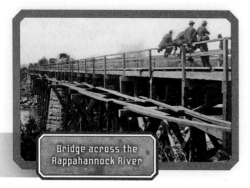

Bridge across the Rappahannock River

Congress were already frustrated that he had wasted so much time on a plan they could no longer use. They became furious when they discovered that Johnston had been fooling the Union army for months. He had held the Union at bay with what looked like rows of cannons, but in fact they were just logs he had painted black! Then the Confederates unveiled their new warship, the CSS *Virginia*, and suddenly all of McClellan's plans to defend Washington seemed equally useless.

On March 11, 1862, Lincoln removed McClellan from his post as general in chief. He left McClellan in charge of the Army of the Potomac, however, and encouraged him to concentrate on the plan to attack and conquer Richmond.

CSS
Virginia

THE PENINSULAR CAMPAIGN

On March 17, McClellan led his Army of the Potomac from Alexandria, Virginia, on what he called the Peninsular Campaign. He had more than one hundred and twenty thousand men at his command.

They advanced up the Virginia Peninsula, but the Confederate army was ready for them. The first city in their path was Yorktown. McClellan had hoped to conquer it quickly. The Confederates dug in and strengthened their defenses. They forced McClellan to lay siege to Yorktown instead. The siege was long and tedious. It kept McClellan's soldiers tied up so they couldn't march on to other cities. To make matters worse, the Confederates used clever tricks to make it seem they had far more troops than they did. They painted logs to look like cannons, just like Johnston had done around

McCLELLAN'S MEN

McClellan put great faith in his Army of the Potomac. He had trained many of the men himself. He believed they could do anything. As he told them in a dispatch three days before the Peninsular Campaign began:

"The moment for action has arrived, and I know that I can trust in you to save our country."

Washington. They marched around quickly to make it seem they had men in more than one place. McClellan already thought the Confederates outnumbered his own soldiers, and these tricks made him even more cautious. Then Johnston withdrew his men toward Williamsburg and Richmond and forced McClellan to chase after him. The Army of the Potomac technically won the Battle of Williamsburg on May 5, but Johnston succeeded in getting many of his troops to Richmond to bolster that city's defenses.

McClellan had hoped to attack Richmond from the James River at the same time his army attacked by land. But Robert E. Lee had installed artillery and a blockade that prevented the Union navy from approaching. Instead, McClellan marched his forces to within four miles of Richmond and set up camp. He planned a major assault for early summer. On May 31 the Confederates attacked. The Union army defended itself and Johnston was wounded, which put Robert E. Lee in command of the Army of Northern Virginia. McClellan did not press his advantage, which gave Lee time to reinforce Richmond and plan a new strategy.

Lee launched a series of attacks against the Union forces. McClellan held his own against the Confederate general but was unwilling to commit his reserves, and finally withdrew from Richmond, admitting he could not take the city. He blamed Lincoln and the War Cabinet for his failure. He accused them of second-guessing him and blocking his leadership.

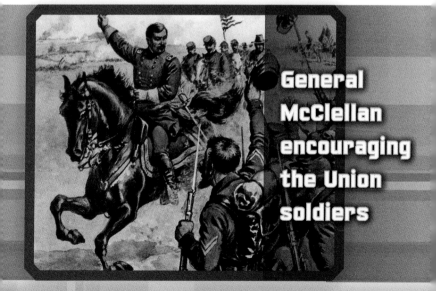

General McClellan encouraging the Union soldiers

In reality much of the failure was due to McClellan's own hesitation. He was an excellent tactician but was unwilling to take the risks necessary for major victories. He also refused to acknowledge orders he did not like, including the new general in chief Henry Halleck's orders for McClellan to reinforce Major General John Pope's attack on Richmond from the northeast. Lee defeated Pope at the Second Battle of Bull Run in late August 1862. The battle was a major blow to the Union and a rallying cry for the Confederacy.

BACK IN COMMAND

Lincoln was forced to admit that neither Halleck nor Pope was an effective military leader. He didn't like

President Lincoln and General McClellan

McClellan's hesitancy or insubordination, but admitted that he was excellent at organizing and encouraging his men. On September 2, Lincoln placed McClellan in charge of the troops and barriers defending Washington, D.C.

Lee launched his Maryland Campaign on September 4, and

McClellan gathered his troops and marched to meet him the following day. Lee had a clever plan to divide his forces into columns, but somehow news of that tactic reached McClellan. He was now confident of victory. As he said in a telegraph to Lincoln:

```
I have the whole rebel force in front of
me, but I am confident, and no time shall
be lost. I think Lee has made a gross mis-
take, and that he will be severely pun-
ished for it. I have all the plans of the
rebels, and will catch them in their own
trap if my men are equal to the emer-
gency.... Will send you trophies.
```

McClellan led his troops to South Mountain, where they pushed through the mountain passes toward Sharpsburg, Maryland, where Lee had gathered his own men. The Union army reached Antietam Creek, east of Sharpsburg, on September 15. The Battle of Antietam occurred two days later. September 17 is still the single bloodiest day in American military history. Twenty-three thousand soldiers were killed, wounded, or missing after twelve hours of battle.

Bodies of Confederate soldiers at Antietam

McClellan didn't use his reserves effectively this time, either. Technically the Union won the battle, since Lee retreated back into Virginia. But they had failed to crush the Confederate army yet again.

Lincoln was displeased—McClellan had won, but only barely, and he had not pursued and destroyed the Confederate forces. On November 5, he removed McClellan from command of the Army of the Potomac and appointed Major General Ambrose Burnside in his place. McClellan was ordered to report to Trenton, New Jersey, and await further orders. None ever came, and McClellan's role in the Civil War was over.

ON TO POLITICS

McClellan blamed Lincoln for many of his problems. He was convinced the war would never end as long as Lincoln was president. In late 1863 McClellan decided that he could not sit by and watch Lincoln ruin the country. He declared himself a Democrat and was nominated to run against Lincoln in the 1864 presidential election. The Democrats hoped that McClellan's status as a war hero and active Union general would win them votes. But their platform called for an end to the war and negotiations with the Confederacy. McClellan could not support these positions. He believed the only way to restore the Union was to win the war completely. It was one of the few things he and Lincoln agreed upon. They just didn't

GENERAL ORDERS
No. 182.

WAR DEPARTMENT,
ADJUTANT GENERAL'S OFFICE,
Washington, November 5, 1862.

By direction of the President of the United States, it is ordered that Major General McCLELLAN be relieved from the command of the Army of the Potomac, and that Major General BURNSIDE take the command of that Army.

BY ORDER OF THE SECRETARY OF WAR:

E. D. TOWNSEND,
Assistant Adjutant General.

General Burnside

agree on how to win the war. But McClellan accepted the nomination.

The Democratic presidential campaign faced several other problems, however. One was the appointment of peace proponent George H. Pendleton as vice presidential candidate. McClellan and Pendleton did not agree, and their differences confused the voters. Another problem was McClellan's own military history. The press played up his hesitation during battle, and the fact that he often had his headquarters set too far away to effectively control the battlefield.

In the end, McClellan's position and reputation didn't matter. When the Union army took Atlanta and forced Lee back to Richmond, Republican victory was assured. Lincoln won the election easily, and began his second term as president. McClellan resigned his military commission on the same day as the election, November 8, 1864.

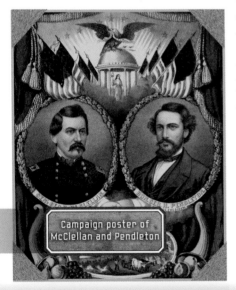

Campaign poster of McClellan and Pendleton

A LIFE LESS MILITARY

McClellan was disappointed by the election results, and by the end of his military career. He took his family to Europe, and they traveled for the next three years. They visited England, Scotland, France, Italy, and Germany. Their son, George Junior, was born on November 23, 1865, while the family was in Dresden, Germany.

After his return, the Democratic Party asked McClellan to consider running for president again, but McClellan declined when he realized it would mean running against the war's final Union general in chief, Ulysses S. Grant. He found work as an engineer instead, and became the superintendent of docks and piers for the city of New York. He resigned that position in 1872 and took his family back to Europe from 1873 to 1875.

In 1877 McClellan was elected governor of New Jersey. He served from 1878 to 1881, and concentrated on reducing taxes and public expenditures, improving education and technical training, and improving the discipline, training, and organization of the state militia.

In 1881 McClellan wrote a book entitled *McClellan's Own Story*. He told about the Civil War and his

McClellan circa 1880

reasons for his actions, defending himself against the many attacks people had made on his leadership. Unfortunately, the only draft was destroyed in a fire. McClellan began to rewrite it, but he had not yet finished it when he died of a heart attack on October 29, 1885. McClellan was buried in Riverview Cemetery in Trenton, New Jersey. The book was published posthumously in 1887.

Some people still blame George McClellan for letting the Civil War drag on so long. But no one can deny that he did what he thought was right. And everyone agrees that he was brilliant at organizing the army. He was also wonderful at caring about the training and welfare of his soldiers. His ideas about training and preparation have helped shape the United States military ever since.

ROBERT E. LEE

ROBERT E. LEE was the general in chief of the Confederate army from 1862 until the end of the Civil War. He is considered one of the finest military minds America ever produced.

A HERO'S SON

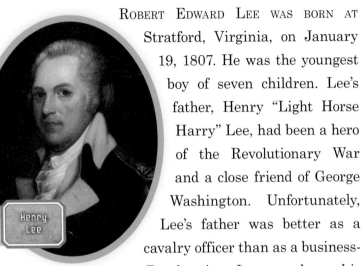

Henry Lee

ROBERT EDWARD LEE WAS BORN AT Stratford, Virginia, on January 19, 1807. He was the youngest boy of seven children. Lee's father, Henry "Light Horse Harry" Lee, had been a hero of the Revolutionary War and a close friend of George Washington. Unfortunately, Lee's father was better as a cavalry officer than as a businessman. By the time Lee was born, his father had gambled away most of the family's money. This example only showed young Lee the importance of focus, discipline, and success. His mother, Ann Hill Carter Lee, taught him those same principles. She also taught him patience and faith.

Henry Lee passed away on March 25, 1818. Lee had barely known his father. Henry Lee had been injured by a mob in Baltimore and spent much of his youngest son's life in the West Indies, where the climate was easier on his health. But his father's death struck Lee hard nonetheless. He had been raised to admire his father's accomplishments and bravery, and those qualities were passed on to all the Lee children.

Lee received an excellent education, thanks to his relatives the Carters. The Carters were a wealthy family with many cousins, and they had established two schools entirely for the family's children. Lee attended Eastern View in Fauquier County with his male cousins. He did well in his classes, though he sometimes became headstrong and arrogant without his mother's constant guidance.

Birthplace of Robert E. Lee

By 1819, however, Lee's life had changed. His mother's health was failing, and she needed constant care. Lee's oldest brother had opened a law office in Washington, D.C., and was rarely home. His other brother had gone to sea with the navy. His sister Mildred had married and moved away. And his sister Ann suffered from poor health and often required medical attention herself. That left Lee to manage the household. He took care of the family's horses, ordered the shopping, and organized their supplies, all while caring for his mother and accompanying her whenever she went out. He did not neglect his lessons despite all these duties. And he still found time to swim and play with other boys in the neighborhood whenever possible.

By the time he was thirteen, Lee had learned everything he could from the tutors at Eastern View. In 1820 he continued his education by entering the Alexandria Academy. He studied there for three years and learned Greek, Latin, and mathematics. But then he had to decide what to do with his life. Should he follow his oldest brother into the law? Should he enter the priesthood? Or should he follow the military path his father had chosen, instead?

Alexandria Academy

TRAINING FOR WAR

Lee decided to follow in his father's footsteps. He would become a soldier! He applied to West Point, and entered the military academy in 1825. Lee was eighteen years old at the time, and already better educated than many of his new classmates. He was also extremely disciplined and self-controlled. He excelled at his courses and at the various physical exercises, and graduated second in his class four years later. Even more impressive was the fact that Lee received no demerits during his entire time at West Point. Students got demerits whenever they did not behave properly, but Lee's behavior was so exemplary that no punishments or warnings were ever needed.

After graduation, Lee was given a commission of second lieutenant in the U.S. Engineer Corps. Years later, George McClellan would follow a similar path, serving in the Engineer Corps before the cavalry and then the volunteer militia and finally facing Lee on the battlefield as general in chief of the Union army.

A LASTING LOVE

As a boy, Lee had often visited Arlington House, the former home of George Washington, with his family. Washington's step-grandson, George Washington Parke Custis, still lived there with his wife and daughter, and the Custises and Lees were good friends.

Mary Randolph Custis Lee

Lee was particularly close to Custis's daughter, Mary Anna Randolph Custis. The two grew to love each other, and in the summer of 1830, Lee proposed. Mary happily accepted, and they were married at Arlington House on June 30, 1831.

OFF TO MEXICO

For the next several years, Lee helped construct military bases. He also worked on several important ports. He helped build the St. Louis waterfront and worked on coastal forts in Brunswick and Savannah. In 1836 he was promoted to first lieutenant, and in 1838 Lee was made a captain. Then, in 1846, war broke out between the United States and Mexico. Lee reported for duty on September 21. It was the first time Lee saw combat, even though he had been in the military for seventeen years.

Lee was initially assigned to scout enemy positions. That was a dangerous job. It meant he had to get close to the enemy in order to see what they were doing. He also worked with other army engineers to build bridges across rivers so that soldiers and cannons could cross safely.

General Winfield Scott was one of the men commanding the American forces. In January 1847 he made Lee a member of his staff. Scott was very impressed by Lee's grasp of tactics. Together they attacked the city of Veracruz. It surrendered in late March. From there they marched toward Mexico City.

Lee distinguished himself during the Mexican-

American War. He won several brevets during the course of the war. Brevets are honorary ranks given for bravery or heroism. Lee was eventually promoted to colonel after the war's climactic Battle of Chapultepec. Lee was wounded during the attack, but American troops conquered the hill and entered Mexico City the same day. The war was over by midnight that night.

A LARGE FAMILY

After the war, Lee returned to engineering work. His father-in-law had invited Lee and his wife to live at Arlington House, and Lee managed to work on projects primarily in Washington and Baltimore so he could stay near home. Lee and Mary's first child, George Washington Custis Lee, was born in 1832. Their second child, Mary Custis Lee, was born in 1835.

Arlington House

William Henry Fitzhugh "Rooney" Lee joined the family in 1837, and Anne Carter Lee was born in 1839. Eleanor Agnes Lee was born in 1841. Robert Edward Lee, Jr., followed her in 1843, and Mildred

Childe Lee came last in 1846. With seven children, Arlington House was never dull!

TEACHING AT WEST POINT

In 1852 Lee was offered the job of superintendent at West Point. That meant he was in charge of the military academy. He served as superintendent for three years. He expanded the number of courses available at the military academy during that time, and improved the education it offered its cadets. Many people felt that Lee had made West Point the equal of the finest military schools in Europe, and many of the cadets who studied under him went on to have impressive military careers. Some of those men, like Lee's nephew Fitzhugh Lee and his own son G. W. Custis Lee, would serve under Lee during the Civil War.

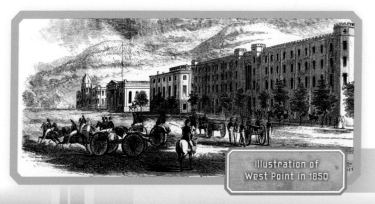

Illustration of
West Point in 1850

TIME IN TEXAS

The United States had annexed Texas from Mexico back in 1845. Mexico had tried to reclaim the territory during the Mexican-American War and had failed. But Mexico was not the only threat to that wide-open stretch of land. Texas covered thousands of miles. The government estimated that nearly thirty thousand Native Americans lived within that area. Most of them resented the United States for trying to take their land. They formed raiding parties and attacked both soldiers and settlers. Something had to be done to protect people.

On March 3, 1855, Congress authorized two new infantry regiments and two new cavalry regiments to help protect Texas and its residents. Lee was transferred from the Engineer Corps to the Second Cavalry, and promoted to the rank of lieutenant colonel under Colonel Albert Sidney Johnston. Johnston, Lee, and their men set out for Camp Cooper in March 1856. It took them almost two weeks to reach the post, which stood alone near the Comanche reservation in what is now Shackelford County, Texas.

Lee didn't mind the quiet. He kept a close eye on the Comanche, watched for any other tribes and raiding parties, explored the area, and supervised his men in their daily activities. In June he led his two cavalry squadrons and two more from Fort Mason and Fort Chadbourne on a sixteen-hundred-mile expedition to the foothills of the Llano Estacado and back in order to scout the headwaters of the Colorado, Brazos, and Wichita rivers. The trip took forty days, and they returned with three Comanche prisoners from an attempted raid.

Soon after that expedition, Lee was recalled to San Antonio. Johnston had been called back to Washington, D.C., and Lee was put in charge of the regiment during Johnston's absence. Lee was forced to return to Washington in October, however, after his father-in-law died. Lee settled his father-in-law's affairs and then returned to his post.

HARPERS FERRY

In October of 1859, Lee was back in Washington on leave to see his family. He was summoned to duty, however, because of a situation in nearby Harpers Ferry, Virginia.

On October 16, abolitionist John Brown and his followers had seized the U.S. Armory and Arsenal at

Harpers Ferry. Brown and his sons had become fugitives in 1856 after killing five men who supported slavery. Brown was determined to establish a colony for runaway slaves, but he needed money and weapons to do that. He decided to capture the arsenal in order to get the weapons he wanted.

Brown and his men had cut the telegraph lines to prevent anyone in Harpers Ferry from calling for help. But a Baltimore and Ohio train had been passing through, and when it reached Baltimore the next day, the conductor alerted the authorities. At the same time, the people of Harpers Ferry turned on Brown and

John Brown on the front page of a newspaper

surrounded the armory so he couldn't escape. Brown took nine men prisoner and holed up in the armory's fire engine house, which was later known as John Brown's Fort.

The authorities knew they needed to stop Brown quickly. They needed to show that people couldn't attack the armory and get away with it. Lee was the closest ranking officer, and had proven himself to be an excellent commander. The government assigned him a detachment of marines and sent them to capture Brown and his followers.

Lee quickly took charge. He closed the town's saloons to stop people from getting drunk and violent. Then he and the marines stormed the fire engine house. They knocked down the door and swept into the small space. Marine Lieutenant Israel Greene wounded Brown and took him prisoner. Most of Brown's men had died during the raid. Several escaped but were captured and brought to trial later. Only a handful escaped completely. Brown stood trial in the Jefferson County

The arsenal at Harpers Ferry burning

Courthouse on October 25. He was found guilty of treason against the Commonwealth of Virginia five days later, and was hanged on December 2. Lee returned to Arlington House and stayed there until February 13, 1860, when he went back to San Antonio to take command of his regiment once more.

DIVIDED LOYALTIES

As 1861 began, the United States grew more and more divided. In early February the states that seceded formed the Confederate States of America. They selected former secretary of war Jefferson Davis as their president. Davis had been a West Point cadet alongside Lee years before.

On February 13 General Scott ordered Lee to return to Washington. He wanted Lee to command the Union army and put down the rebellion.

Lee was torn. He was a loyal American citizen, but he was also a loyal Virginian. He had been born and raised in that state. America was still only a loose alliance, and each state had its own identity. Though the states worked together, each state put its own interests first. And people usually thought of their state's well-being first, too.

In spite of his desire to protect the Union, Lee turned down Scott's offer, then resigned from the army altogether.

It was a shocking decision, and many Union commanders and politicians called Lee a traitor. But Lee had been raised to believe in the honor of his family and his home state, and felt he was too tied to Virginia to ever stand against it.

Lee made his way back home to Arlington, and then continued on to Richmond. The state capital had become the capital of the Confederacy as well, and Jefferson Davis had established his headquarters there. Lee felt honor-bound to offer his services to Davis, and the Confederate president was only too happy to accept. Davis made Lee a major general in the Virginian forces. A few weeks later, he promoted

LEE'S DECISION

In January 1861 Lee wrote to his eldest son: "I can anticipate no greater calamity for the country than the dissolution of the Union. It would be an accumulation of all the evils we complain of, and I am willing to sacrifice everything but honor for its preservation."

Lee to brigadier general, which was the highest rank available. Lee was willing to do his duty, but hoped he would never have to take arms against the Union officers who had recently been his fellow soldiers.

FIRST CONFLICTS

Initially, Lee served as a military advisor to Davis. He did lead the defense of Virginia, but McClellan's Union soldiers were able to fight past Lee's troops and secure the western portion of the state, which later became the separate state of West Virginia.

The defeat made Lee doubt his ability to lead. He returned his attention to advising Davis on military strategy. He also worked to fortify and defend the Atlantic coast in case the Union tried to attack from that direction. Those same defenses stopped McClellan's plan to invade Virginia by boat, and blocked the Union navy from attacking.

When McClellan's Army of the Potomac marched toward Richmond in the spring of 1862, Lee was there to man the city's defenses. His former fellow engineer Joseph E. Johnston was in command of the Confederate army itself. But Johnston was wounded at the Battle of Fair Oaks on May 31, 1862. Lee was given command of the Army of Northern Virginia in his place. Lee knew he couldn't match McClellan's numbers, so he relied upon aggression instead. He launched a series of attacks, known as the Seven Days' Battle, and slowly but surely forced McClellan to retreat.

General Lee and Johnston

THE ARMY OF NORTHERN VIRGINIA

Lee led the Confederate army for the next three years. He proved himself a master of strategy. On August 29, the armies fought for a second time at Bull Run. The previous encounter there had ended in a victory for the Confederates. This time was much the same. Lee's subordinates General Thomas J. "Stonewall" Jackson and General James Longstreet outfought General John Pope's larger army and forced the Union soldiers to retreat to Washington.

Lee and Davis agreed that now was the time to push northward and take Washington, D.C. If they could conquer the Union capital, they could force President

Painting of Stonewall Jackson

Lincoln to recognize the Confederate States of America as a separate nation and end the war once and for all. Lee led his forces into Pennsylvania and marched toward Washington.

On September 4, 1862, Lee and his army invaded the North and headed toward Harpers Ferry, the same armory he had rescued from John Brown three years earlier. McClellan was back in command of the Union army and pursued Lee. The two armies clashed at Antietam on September 17.

Lee was unable to overpower the larger Union force this time. By nightfall more than twenty-six thousand men lay dead on the field, and Lee was forced to withdraw. He and his army retreated to Virginia. The Army of the Potomac pursued them, but without their commander—Lincoln replaced McClellan with General Ambrose E. Burnside in November. On December 13 Burnside led the Union troops against Lee's men at Fredericksburg, Virginia. But the Confederates had chosen their position well. They had dug in on Marye's Heights, and repelled fourteen assaults without budging. The Union lost more than twelve thousand men, and was finally forced to yield Fredericksburg and return across the Potomac.

CONTINUED CONFLICT

In May 1863 Lee and his most trusted officer, General Stonewall Jackson, divided their forces to strike Union General Joe Hooker's army on two sides during the Battle of Chancellorsville. Hooker had more men but couldn't keep his soldiers united, and fell before the double attack. Sadly, Jackson was fatally wounded during the conflict, after being accidentally shot by his own men. Though they won the battle, the Confederates suffered almost as many losses as the Union army.

In June Lee led seventy-five thousand soldiers in a second attempt to invade the North. They crossed into Pennsylvania and swept upward. But the new Union commander, George G. Meade, met Lee at Gettysburg on July 1, and the Battle of Gettysburg raged over the next three days. When it was over, Lee had been defeated, and was forced to retreat to Virginia once again.

To make matters worse, on July 4 Union General Ulysses S. Grant and his Army of the Tennessee had conquered the Confederate stronghold at Vicksburg, Virginia. Vicksburg had been the last Confederate fort along the Mississippi River, and the Union now controlled that waterway completely. This cut the Confederacy in two and deprived Lee of aid from the western states.

At the start of the year, Lincoln had issued his Emancipation Proclamation, freeing the Confederates' slaves and encouraging them to enlist in the Union army. A few months later, Congress enacted a draft. These two acts expanded the Union army, which had already outnumbered the Confederates. Now Lee faced waves of fresh young men, while his own soldiers were wounded and growing tired and weak.

Battle at Vicksburg

On October 16, 1863, President Lincoln placed Grant in control of the Union's armies in the west. Grant had already proven to be a challenging opponent. He and Lee had learned from several of the same men, including General Winfield Scott during the Mexican-American War. One of Grant's first acts as general in chief was to break the Confederate army that had been holding Chattanooga, Tennessee. The tide of the war was beginning to turn against the Confederacy.

THE WAR'S END

On March 9, 1864, Lincoln made Grant the general in chief of the Union armies. General William T. Sherman took over as commander in the west. Grant quickly coordinated his forces, and on May 4 he led an army of one hundred and twenty thousand soldiers against Lee's Army of Northern Virginia outside Richmond. Lee had only sixty-four thousand soldiers under his command at the time. Meanwhile, Sherman led another hundred thousand men south toward Atlanta to battle Johnston's Army of Tennessee. By June the Union forces had closed in on Petersburg and surrounded Lee's men. On September 2 Sherman captured Atlanta—the news helped Lincoln win reelection against George McClellan. On December 16 Union General George H. Thomas destroyed Confederate General Hood's army at Nashville, ending the Confederate Army of Tennessee. Five days later Sherman reached Savannah. Lee was running out of men, generals, and safe havens.

General William T. Sherman

Lee's surrender in Virginia

On March 25, 1865, Lee led his Army of Northern Virginia on its final attack. They tried to break through Grant's lines at Petersburg. The battle lasted four hours, but in the end, Grant held firm. Lee was still trapped.

A week later, on April 2, Grant advanced and broke through Lee's defenses. Lee was forced to flee Petersburg. The Confederates abandoned Richmond. The next day, Union troops raised the American flag over the former Confederate capitol.

Lee had brought the remains of his army with him when he left Petersburg, but there was nowhere left to go. On April 9, 1865, he surrendered his forces to Grant at Appomattox Court House in Virginia.

AFTER THE WAR

Lee had never wanted a war. He had defended his state as best he could, but he was just as happy to see the war over. He was also both an officer and a gentleman. Even if he had been upset about the outcome of the war, Lee was not the type to be difficult and make trouble after the matter had been settled.

For the first few months after the war, Lee lived quietly, letting tempers cool and conflicts fade. Some people wanted to charge him with treason, but the

LEE'S THOUGHTS ON SLAVERY

People often assume that Lee was proslavery because he commanded the Confederate forces. In fact, he did not feel that way at all. As he stated on May 1, 1870, a few short months before his death:

"So far from engaging in a war to perpetuate slavery, I am rejoiced that Slavery is abolished. I believe it will be greatly for the interest of the South. So fully am I satisfied of this that I would have cheerfully lost all that I have lost by the war, and have suffered all that I have suffered to have this object attained."

Washington College in 1867

government was eager to put the entire war behind them and didn't want to drag things out with charges on either side. Besides, many people still considered Lee a hero from the Mexican-American War and from the incident at Harpers Ferry. Charging him with treason would only have upset people all over again. Lee did have his civil rights suspended, which meant he could not vote or receive the normal protections of an American citizen in legal matters. He accepted the punishment with good grace.

Of course, Lee could not rejoin the army. He had no idea what to do with himself now that his military career was over. Fortunately, in August 1865 he was offered a new position. He had been superintendent of

Lee between 1860 and 1865

West Point for three happy years, and now he was given the chance to run another school. This time it was Washington College in Lexington, Virginia. The school offered Lee the position of president, and he was happy to accept.

Lee served as the college's president from September 1865 until his death on October 12, 1870. He was buried on the college grounds. Years later, the school was renamed Washington and Lee University in his honor. And in 1975 President Gerald Ford officially pardoned Lee and restored his American citizenship.

To many, Robert E. Lee is the perfect example of the Southern gentleman. He believed in honor, discipline, loyalty, and hard work. He made difficult choices and accepted the consequences. He was a brilliant commander and an excellent soldier, but he was also an honest and honorable man who only wanted to fulfill his responsibilities as best he could.

MATHEW BRADY

MATHEW BRADY was one of the most famous and successful photographers in America. Many consider him to be the father of photojournalism. When he was alive, he was famous for his portraits, but today he is best known for his photos documenting the Civil War.

MURKY BEGINNINGS

VERY LITTLE IS KNOWN ABOUT MATHEW B. BRADY'S childhood. As he stated in an interview with the *World:* "I go back to near 1823–'24; . . . my birthplace was Warren County, N.Y., in the woods about Lake George, and . . . my father was an Irishman."

Brady grew up in Saratoga Springs in upstate New York. He had sharp eyes and clever hands, and learned the art of manufacturing jewelry cases. Brady was a teen when he met the painter William Page. Page took a liking to Brady and began teaching him how to paint. When Page went to New York City in 1841 to study at Morse's National Academy of Design, he brought Brady with him.

Louis
Daguerre

Professor Samuel F. B. Morse later invented the telegraph, but at the time he was just developing the alphabet for that device while still teaching art. Morse also had a second school, and it was this institute that would change Brady's life. The school was based on the work of a man named Louis Daguerre, who was working on a new way to develop images. Daguerre and his partner, Nicéphore Niépce, had created a method that used chemicals to fix an image upon specially treated paper. The result was called a daguerreotype. It was an early form of photograph.

Brady studied at Morse's school of daguerreotypy. He studied the photography and soon became an expert at the technique himself. In 1844 Brady opened his own Daguerreian Miniature Gallery, where he took and exhibited his daguerreotypes. The technique was still

EARLY PHOTOGRAPHY

The camera obscura had been invented in Italy in the late 1500s. It was a large box with a lens on one side and an eyepiece opposite it. Objects were examined through the lens, and the light was then focused and reflected through a series of mirrors within.

In 1826 Niépce found a way to take an image using light and certain chemicals. Eleven years later, Daguerre improved the process. He used thin sheets of silver-plated copper and iodine fumes. Then he developed the plates with mercury vapors. The process took only forty minutes, and the images were sharper and clearer and lasted longer than Niépce's had. By 1841 Daguerre had shortened the processing time.

very new, and Brady was one of the few who had mastered it. Word of his gallery got around, and soon his pieces were in high demand.

AWARDS AND ACCLAIM

In 1845, Brady entered the American Institute's daguerreotype competition. He won first prize in two different classes. In 1851 he went to England. Queen Victoria had annouced the first World's Fair in London, and wanted daguerreotypes to feature as a major exhibit. Brady displayed his work there, and entered his work in the competition at the World's Fair's Crystal Palace Exhibition. He won first prize there as well. That same year, the *Photographic Art-Journal* began—the magazine's first issue described Brady as the "fountainhead" of the new profession of portrait photography.

BRADY'S PURPOSE

Mathew Brady took the job of photographing people very seriously. As he explained it:
   "From the first, I regarded myself as under obligation to my country to preserve the faces of its historic men and mothers."

The Crystal Palace in 1851

Most daguerreotypes were portraits at this time. "And portrait photographers made their living by photographing the wealthy and the famous. The wealthy paid a great deal for their daguerreotypes, but celebrities were even better. The photographer could sell prints of the same photograph to magazines, newspapers, and people who wanted portraits of these famous men and women. Daguerreotypes sold for three to five dollars each back then, which was an impressive sum. Brady quickly acquired an impressive reputation that

Edgar
Allan Poe

helped him convince many famous people to sit for portraits at his gallery studio. He took photographs of former president Andrew Jackson just before he died, and managed to capture acclaimed writer Edgar Allan Poe as well. He photographed President John Taylor, who had served as vice president and took office after William Henry Harrison died in office in 1841. In 1860, when the Prince of Wales came to the United States, he made a point of visiting Brady's studio for a portrait. Part of the appeal was that Brady took real care with each sitting. He believed he had a serious responsibility with each photograph.

Brady later said that his lack of confidence actually helped him get celebrities to sit for him. He was quiet and patient, and not brash like so many men. Rather than insist upon sittings, he politely asked or invited people to have him take their portraits. Whatever the reason, more and more people sought him out as his fame grew.

APPEARING IN PRINT

Up until this time, illustrations for books and magazines and newspapers were hand-drawn or done as woodcuts so they could be turned into prints. But daguerreotypes provided a clearer, cleaner image and could produce sharper prints. They were perfect for illustrations, provided you could afford them. In 1846 Brady was offered the chance to provide images for an entire book. Eliza Farnham was a scientist studying prisoners. She asked Brady to make portraits of the prisoners she discussed in her book *Rationale of Crime*. Brady was happy to contribute. It was one of the first books to use daguerreotypes for the illustrations.

Four years later, Brady decided to try his hand at producing a book. It was called *Gallery of Illustrious Americans* and had twelve lithographs made from his daguerreotypes. The book included portraits of former president Zachary Taylor, statesman and speaker Daniel Webster, President

Zachary Taylor

Millard Fillmore, U.S. army general Winfield Scott, and naturalist and bird expert John James Audubon. Unfortunately, the book did not do well. Brady's own galleries were partially to blame. Many people decided it was more practical to visit his gallery and admire the pictures for free. The book was expensive, because it had cost a great deal to produce. Brady needed to sell a lot of copies to cover what he had spent to produce the book, but most people couldn't or wouldn't pay that much for a handful of pictures.

HAPPY COMPANIONSHIP

The year 1851 was a good year for Brady for two reasons. He won first prize at the World's Fair in London and he was a newlywed. Brady had met Juliette Handy at his studio, and had instantly fallen in love. The two were married shortly before his trip to London, and applied for passports together. It was a happy time for Brady. He was married to a wonderful woman, and his career was starting to gain international attention.

A SECOND SET OF EYES

Photography requires a sharp eye that can see not only detail but composition and expression. But after

Brady's trip to England, he started having more trouble seeing details. As a child he'd had an eye condition, described as "a violent inflammation of the eyes," and almost lost his sight. Though he'd received medical treatment in Albany, Brady's eyes had never fully recovered from that illness. By the 1850s his eyesight was so bad he could no longer take pictures by himself. He needed someone to help, to act as his eyes.

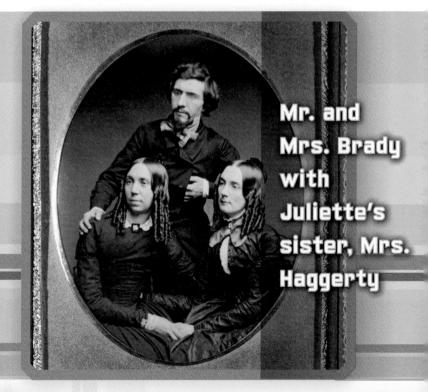

Mr. and Mrs. Brady with Juliette's sister, Mrs. Haggerty

He found that help in a young man named Alexander Gardner. Gardner was an excellent photographer in his own right. He was also an expert at the new collodion photography process. This technique used wet photographic plates and was rapidly replacing daguerreotypes as the leading form of photography. The biggest advantage of the new process was its ability to produce an unlimited number of perfect paper prints. Brady made Gardner his chief assistant, and relied upon him heavily. But the compositions were usually still Brady's invention.

TWICE AS MUCH

In 1856 Brady opened a second studio. This one was on Pennsylvania Avenue NW in Washington, D.C., halfway between the White House and the Capitol building. Now he had easier access to the nation's leading politicians. He photographed presidents, generals, and many others. Brady also figured out how to carry his photographic equipment in a wagon, so he could go anywhere he needed to take a picture. It was a new idea, and allowed him to photograph landscapes and local events. He could also take pictures of people in their own element instead of in the neutral surroundings of his studio. A person's home or office said a lot about their character. Brady could now include that in his photographs, so that the entire image helped tell a story.

In 1858 Brady put Gardner in charge of his Washington, D.C., gallery. He had trained several other young men to assist him, including a very talented apprentice named Timothy O'Sullivan. Between them, they ran the two galleries and continued to provide portraits, landscape photos, and event photos as required. It was Gardner who showed Brady how to produce images in large quantities. This allowed them to produce photo albums for entire families. Many of their customers asked to include images of famous men and women as well.

SWAYING THE VOTE

Brady was also more than happy to accept assignments directly from newspapers and magazines. They sent people to him, or asked him to bring his portable equipment and take someone's photograph at an event or a particular place. Then those photographic plates could be used to produce wood types, which could then be placed in the papers.

Other photographers were available, but Brady was

very much in demand. He had a real talent for setting the scene. He could take a photograph that captured the best qualities of the subject. It was a true art, far more than just snapping a picture.

The pictures they saw heavily influenced people. The right photograph could make a man look like a villain or a hero. It could also convince people to vote for a politician by making him look honest and trustworthy and capable.

Perhaps the most influential picture Brady ever took was of a young politician in 1861. The man was

Abraham Lincoln in 1861

a former senator from Illinois. He was running for president of the United States. The man had been invited to speak to the Republican Party at Cooper Union on February 28. Brady was on hand to take his photograph. He captured the man's long, lanky figure and his plain, honest face. The man in the photograph looked strong and noble and determined. The speech was a wild success. So was the photograph, which was used in many magazines across the country. Everyone who saw it agreed that this was a man who could be president. Abraham Lincoln would later say, "Brady and the Cooper Institute made me President."

IMAGES OF WAR

When the Civil War began in 1861, Brady decided that he needed to document the entire conflict. It was a mad scheme. There were hundreds of thousands of soldiers, and they were marching all over the United States. How could anyone hope to photograph any of the battles, much less all of them?

There was also the danger. These men were fighting for their lives! Who was going to pose for a photograph while dodging bullets and sabers?

And there was the cost. How much would Brady spend to traipse across the country and photo-graph these events? Who would want to buy prints of such horrific scenes?

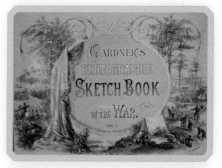

But Brady was deter-mined. As he told friends,

"I had to go. A spirit in my feet said 'Go,' and I went."

He did not go alone, however. He organized an entire troop of photographers to accompany him and to travel to the battles he could not reach himself. There were at least twenty teams in all. Each of them had a wagon filled with photography equipment, because they had to develop the photographs on the spot. Brady provided the equipment and the wagons. But for protection, they were left with whatever personal weapons they possessed and whatever luck they might have.

Soldiers' graves at the Bull Run battlefield

RUNNING AT BULL RUN

Brady's first outing was to follow the Union army to Manassas, Virginia. He had two wagons and his friends Dick McCormick, Ned House, and Al Waud to help. There he witnessed the disastrous First Battle of Bull

Run. One observer noted that Brady and his men showed more courage than many of the army officers that day. He and his assistants stayed and took photographs when many of the soldiers had left. When the last of the Union forces fled, Brady realized his life was in just as much danger. He and his assistants ran as fast as they could. They managed to escape to safety, but they lost the wagons. For three days they wandered, lost and starving. Fortunately, Brady managed to save the photographic plates themselves.

He continued to organize his photographers and go on outings himself throughout the war. Most of the soldiers were only too happy to pose for them. So were the officers, including General George B. McClellan and his staff. Many had gotten portraits done before they'd left for war, looking handsome in their new uniforms. But this was different. These were real images of the war, and they showed the men dirty and tired and wounded. But it also showed their pride and their courage. The images were spellbinding.

In 1862 Brady put on the first exhibition of his Civil War photographs. They were of the battle at Antietam, and they were shocking. The sign on the door to his New York gallery simply read "The Dead of Antietam."

Bodies of deceased soldiers at Antietam

The images were terrible but captivating. They showed the people of New York just what really happened on the battlefield.

Brady's fame and connections also served him well. He was able to take a photograph of Robert E. Lee in 1865 in Richmond, Virginia, a week after Lee surrendered the Army of Northern Virginia to Union general Ulysses S. Grant. That surrender effectively ended the war. Lee was not eager to pose for a photograph, and most photographers would have respected that wish and left the defeated general alone. But Brady had known Lee since the Mexican-American War. He also knew Mrs. Lee, and appealed to her. She helped convince her husband to take the photograph, for the sake of history. It is a powerful image, showing Lee's sorrow and fatigue. He is wearing the same new Confederate uniform he wore when meeting Grant.

A DESPERATE GAMBLE

Brady had known he could sell images of the war's major figures, like Union general Grant and Confederate general Lee. And those pictures sold quite well. Some of the prints of soldiers also sold, mainly to their families and friends. Other customers were not interested in buying images of the dead on the battlefield. Nor did most people want to buy a large collection of the depressing war photographs.

Robert E. Lee in 1865

But Brady had never expected people to buy those pictures. He had a different goal in mind. He was chronicling the events of the war, from start to finish.

Brady had assumed the Union would win the Civil

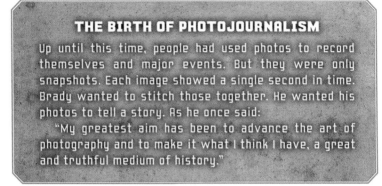

THE BIRTH OF PHOTOJOURNALISM

Up until this time, people had used photos to record themselves and major events. But they were only snapshots. Each image showed a single second in time. Brady wanted to stitch those together. He wanted his photos to tell a story. As he once said:

"My greatest aim has been to advance the art of photography and to make it what I think I have, a great and truthful medium of history."

War. And he felt sure the government would want a record of events afterward. That was where his photographs came in. He intended to sell them to the government as a single unified collection. It would be the largest, most comprehensive photography set ever produced.

But when he offered his photographs to the government, they refused. They didn't want the grisly reminder of what had happened. Everyone just wanted to put the war behind them.

Brady was devastated. He had assembled more than ten thousand negatives and had spent more than one hundred thousand dollars. It was a fortune, and had taken nearly all of his money. He had assumed the government would pay handsomely for the set, and he would not only make his money back but also collect a tidy profit. Instead he found himself almost broke. To make matters worse, no one wanted the photographs he had risked his life to take. Later in life, he said:

> No one will ever know what I went through to secure those negatives. The world can never appreciate it. It changed the whole course of my life.

Brady next to the tree with General Burnside in Virginia

STRUGGLING TO SURVIVE

Brady was forced to close his New York gallery in 1873 to pay off some of his debts. E. and H. T. Anthony, brothers who bought and sold photographic materials, seized a set of Brady's war negatives as payment for some of his other debts. Brady had sold them negatives in exchange for supplies throughout the war, and they had already published many of those images in small sets.

Another collection of negatives was auctioned off when Brady couldn't afford to store them anymore. They wound up being purchased by the War Department.

To make matters worse, Juliette Handy Brady died in 1887. Brady was crushed. Without the love of his life, he found it even harder to continue.

Brady kept his Washington gallery and returned to portraits as a way to survive. His photograph of Clara Barton, the best-known picture of her, was taken after the war. He photographed Frederick Douglass many years later.

In 1875 the government changed its mind and offered to buy Brady's remaining plates. But they only paid him twenty-five thousand dollars for the

Brady's New York gallery

negatives. That was less than a fourth of what he had spent during the war!

A SAD END

In 1895 Brady was living in a rooming house. He was old, alone, and broke, but he refused to give up. He decided the time had come to show his Civil War photographs once more. Brady began preparing a series of slide lectures. But his health was failing, and he fell ill before he could finish. Because he was too poor to afford private care, Brady was taken to the charity ward of the Presbyterian Hospital in New York. The doctors did the best they could, but were limited in what they could offer a man with no money to pay for care. Brady died in the hospital on January 15, 1896.

POSTHUMOUS RECOGNITION

Years later, people began to take an interest in the Civil War again. This was a new generation who had not experienced the war themselves. They wanted to learn about this period of American history. The government agreed that it was important to remember what had happened, and to honor the young men who had given their lives for their country. And then the

Mathew Brady in 1889

government remembered Brady's photographs.

The Anthony Company sold its set of Brady's negatives to an amateur historian named Frederick Hill Meserve at the end of the century. In 1981 Meserve's family put the collection up for sale. The National Portrait Gallery bought all five thousand of them, and placed them with the Smithsonian Institution.

Brady's collection is now divided between the National Archives and the Library of Congress in Washington, D.C. It is an amazing photographic record. Thanks to Brady's work, people can see exactly what the war was like. They can see the real people involved. And they can see history in the making. Brady's desire to preserve history came true. Sadly, it happened too late for him to see how much people appreciate all of his efforts. He is now better known for his Civil War images than for all the portraits he did put together. The Brady Collection is still considered a national treasure.

CONCLUSION

IT CAN BE AMAZING HOW PEOPLE ARE CONNECTED, AND how those connections affect the world around them. If Mathew Brady had not taken Lincoln's photograph outside Cooper Union, Lincoln might not have become president. Would the Civil War still have happened? Probably. Slavery was not an issue that was going to go away, and the southern states were not going to give up their slaves without a fight. But without Lincoln in office, Frederick Douglass might not have found a sympathetic ear. The Union might never have agreed to allow black men to join the army. And without those extra troops, George McClellan might not have been able to block Robert E. Lee's attack on Washington, D.C. If his defenses had failed, Lee and the Confederates might have taken Washington, and ended the war right there. Or perhaps without the black soldiers, the Union might not have been able to end the war as early as it did. Lee might not have surrendered at Appomattox. If Lee had not surrendered then, Lincoln might have died before the end of the war. He might never have had the chance to ask Clara Barton to look into the missing soldiers. Barton might not have found all those lost and wounded men, and the country might never have known the full extent of the war's casualties. They might have thought the war was less severe than it was. Which might have meant they never bought Brady's Civil War photographs. And then we might never have known what the war was really like, or the faces of the people so closely involved—people including Lincoln, Douglass, Barton, McClellan, and Lee.

All of these people are connected. They all had a part to play in the war, and in its aftermath. And seeing those parts, learning about these people, helps us put all the pieces together. It's easy to study one aspect of the war. But by looking at these different sides we can see what really happened. We can learn about why it happened, and why people did what they did. Each of these people—Lincoln, Douglass, Barton, McClellan, Lee, and Brady—did what they thought was best. They stood up for their beliefs and their ideals, and they tried to help the people around them. Their actions helped shape the American Civil War, and by studying their actions we can understand a bit of what they went through, and admire their bravery and determination. We can see that each of them, in their own way, was a hero of the Civil War.

MAP 157

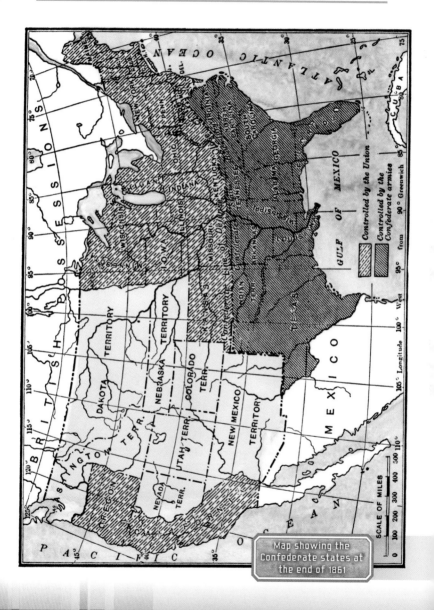

Map showing the Confederate states at the end of 1861

BOOKS

Barton, William E. *The Life of Clara Barton: Founder of the American Red Cross*. New York: AMS Press, 1969.

Donald, David Herbert. *Lincoln*. New York: Touchstone, 1995.

Douglass, Frederick. *The Life and Times of Frederick Douglass*. Dover: Dover Publications, 2003. First published 1881 by Park Publishing Co.

——. *My Bondage and My Freedom*. New York: Penguin Classics, 2003. First published 1855 by Miller, Orton & Mulligan.

——. *Narrative of the Life of Frederick Douglass: An American Slave, Written by Himself*. New York: St. Martin's, 2002. First published 1845 by Dover.

Fellman, Michael. *The Making of Robert E. Lee*. New York: Random House, 2000.

Freeman, Douglas Southall. *Lee*. Abridgment by Richard Harwell. New York: Collier Books, 1993.

Lincoln, Abraham. *Abraham Lincoln: His Speeches and Writings*. Edited by Roy P. Basler. New York: Da Capo Press, 1990. First published 1946 by World Pub. Co.

Panzer, Mary. *Mathew Brady and the Image of History*. Washington, DC: Smithsonian Institution Press, 1997.

Pryor, Elizabeth Brown. *Clara Barton: Professional Angel*. Philadelphia: University of Pennsylvania Press, 1987.

Rafuse, Ethan S. *McClellan's War: The Failure of Moderation in the Struggle for the Union*. Bloomington: Indiana University Press, 2005.

Sears, Stephen W. *George B. McClellan: The Young Napoleon*. New York: Da Capo Press, 1999. First published 1988 by Ticknor & Fields.

Thomas, Emory M. *Robert E. Lee: A Biography*. New York: W. W. Norton & Co., 1995.

ARTICLES

Kendrick, Paul, and Stephen Kendrick. "Lincoln & Douglass." *American Heritage Magazine* 58 (Winter 2009): 36. http://www.american heritage.com/articles/magazine/ah/2009/6/2009_6_36.shtml.

"M. B. Brady: Phrenological Character and Biography." *American Phrenological Journal* 27, no. 5 (May 1858): 65–67. http://www.daguerre.org/resource/texts/brady_phreno.html.

"Still Taking Pictures: Brady, the Grand Old Man of American Photography." *The World*, April 12, 1891, 26. http://www2.iath .virginia.edu/spirit_trouts/mnookin/brady.html.

WEBSITES

http://clarabartonbirthplace.org/site/
http://encyclopediavirginia.org/McClellan_George_B_1826-1885
http://memory.loc.gov/ammem/cwphtml/cwbrady.html
http://memory.loc.gov/ammem/doughtml/doughome.html
http://www.civilwar.com/
http://www.civil-war.net/
http://www.essortment.com/all/abrahamlincoln_rrzw.htm
http://www.mathewbrady.com/
http://www.mrlincolnswhitehouse.org/inside asp?ID=38&subjectID=2
http://www.nps.gov/archive/gett/getttour/main-ms.htm
http://www.nps.gov/clba/
http://www.sonofthesouth.net/leefoundation/About%
    20the%20General.htm
http://www.whitehouse.gov/about/presidents/abrahamlincoln

INDEX